LOTHIAN

Edited by Lucy Jenkins

First published in Great Britain in 1999 by
YOUNG WRITERS
Remus House,
Coltsfoot Drive,
Woodston,
Peterborough, PE2 9JX
Telephone (01733) 890066

HB ISBN 0 75431 620 3
SB ISBN 0 75431 621 1

FOREWORD

Young Writers have produced poetry books in conjunction with schools for over eight years; providing a platform for talented young people to shine. This year, the Celebration 2000 collection of regional anthologies were developed with the millennium in mind.

With the nation taking stock of how far we have come, and reflecting on what we want to achieve in the future, our anthologies give a vivid insight into the thoughts and experiences of the younger generation.

We were once again impressed with the quality and attention to detail of every entry received and hope you will enjoy the poems we have decided to feature in *Celebration 2000 Lothian* for many years to come.

CONTENTS

Colinton Primary School

Stephanie Wood	85
Cameron Gaff	85
Rachael Mary Kirk	86
Michael Macfarlane	86
James John Carr	87
Muzamel Amjed	87
Scott Dowd	88
Daniel Rhymes	88
Murray Poole	89

Cramond Primary School

Fraser Pirie	89
Mike Nowiszewski	90
Katie Buchanan	90
Naomi Gibson	91
Hari Sukarjo	92
Catherine Atterton	92
Ailsa Jack	93
Stuart Brown	93
Craig Macpherson	94
Lauren Chornogubsky	94
Gemma Thomson	95
Robert Lyon	95
Desmond Doran	95
Calum Boyce	96
Michael Logue	96
James Macnaughton	97
Aaron Foreman	97
Alex Targowski	97
Katherine Goudie	98
Omeair Saeed	98
Joanna Highton	99
Liam Blaikie	99
Daniel Guild	100
Jamie Hamilton	100
Helen Robson	101
Geoff Melrose	101

Prestonfield School

St Mary's RC Primary School, Bonnyrigg

St Matthew's Primary School, Rosewell

St Peter's RC Primary School, Edinburgh

The Poems

20TH CENTURY HIGHLIGHTS

Clatter! Bang!
As the bombs fall.
Children queue to see 'Snow White'
In their houses people sing and
dance to the 'Sound of Music'.
Our King goes with Mrs Simpson.

Oh no, the Tacoma Bridge collapses.
The World War II continues
then ends in 1945.
Anne Frank's diary was published
What a book!

Elvis Presley is the spot of
conversation.
The Coronation takes place
and Space Age too.

Give your hands a rest with a
new washing machine.
Buy your fabulous mini skirt,
And don't forget your Beatles record.

Are you a test tube baby?
Britain joins Europe
And 'Grease' is lightning.

Ashley Dunsmore (11)
Balbardie Primary School

20TH CENTURY HIGHLIGHTS

The 30's was a sad time
because the war started.

The 40's were the roaring years
with the Tacoma Bridge falling down.

The 50's were good. Lots of years
with Elvis, TV and the 'Festival' arrived.

In the 60's England won the World Cup
and the first man went into space.

The 70's was a sad decade for some
Both Kennedy and Lennon were assassinated
Good news too!
The first test tube baby was born.
A girl too!

Neil Butler (11)
Balbardie Primary School

MILLENNIUM

M illennium comes each thousand years,
I t is a very exciting time for us,
L et's all have a party,
L et's sing and dance all night long,
E veryone is celebrating,
N obody is sad,
N ew millennium coming in,
I n this world we're glad to see this event,
U tter happiness around the word
M illennium!

Terry Whiteside (10)
Balbardie Primary School

POEMS FROM THE 20TH CENTURY

The 30's were sad with
World War II beginning.
There were bombings,
buildings were destroyed and
people were killed.
People were starving.
Evacuees were leaving their
families for safe villages.

The 'Roaring 40's' -
The Tacoma Bridge collapsed.
World War II ended at last.
Anne Frank's diary was published
and was a great seller.

The 'Fab 50's' were a treat
with the 'king', Elvis Presley
who broke many girls' hearts.
He sang love songs and 'rock and roll'.

The 'Swinging 60's' with washing
machines, miniskirts so short.
'Flower Power' was in the brain
with daisy chains and headbands.

The 'Groovy 70's' were kind and
gentle with Mother Teresa who
helped everyone. The first test tube
baby was the only one for that mum.

These were the highlights of the 20th Century.

Jennifer Thomson (12)
Balbardie Primary School

THE 20TH CENTURY

In the 30's there were films
such as 'Snow White' and
'Gone With The Wind'.
The war also started and
people were scared.
Our King, then Edward, ran
off with Mrs. Simpson.

Then in the 40's the
Tacoma Bridge collapsed.
After that the war ended,
and a little Jewish girl who
had hidden during the war,
her diary was published.
Her name was Anne Frank.

In the 50's Elvis Presley
became famous.
People called this era
'the famous fifties'. TV
came along and people
were excited.

In the 60's people had flowers
and had 'flower power'.
And then the Beatles
became famous.
England won the World Cup
and made history.

In the 70's the Monkees
were the craze as well as
Bay City Rollers and all
that tartan. One of the greatest
films of all time came out
'Star Wars'.

Ross Taggart (11)
Balbardie Primary School

GOING TO THE PAST

We're going to the past,
Very very fast.

The 30's had a passion for fashion,
Laurel and Hardy,
to the Dandy.

From the 30's to the 40's
Churchill vs Hitler
The ball-point pen
to the Number 10.

From the 40's to the 50's
Elvis loves his pelvis
The Queen is crowned,
Hula hoops are sound.

From the 50's to the 60's
The Beatles vs the Monkees
England vs West Germany.

From the 60's to the 70's
Punks vs hippies
'Night Fever' to 'Grease'.

Andrew Weir (11)
Balbardie Primary School

20TH CENTURY POEM 1930'S-1970'S

In the 30's the war began
with Hitler and the Germans
trying to rule the land.
Peace also came as a film came out.
Their first film ever and it was
a fairy tale called 'Snow White'.

In the middle of the 40's the
war ended
Sadness hadn't stopped as loved
ones had died.
Anne Frank's diary was also
published with sad diary entries
telling about her life.

The 50's were swinging with Elvis
Presley's 'Blue Suede Shoes' 'Jail
House Rock' and 'Hound Dog'.
These were some famous hits for him.
The TV was new and exciting and
everybody wanted one.
Electricity was wonderful as people
could do some wonderful things
with it.

60's were fashionable with miniskirts
galore and huge knee-high
boots in black or white.
Washing machines were invented
and popular they were too
to ease the strain off women.

Now we are at the 70's when
'Grease' the film came out.
Gel hair was so popular just
like the main characters Danny
and Sandy.
Britain came to their senses at
last as they joined up with Europe.

Pamela Bell (12)
Balbardie Primary School

20TH CENTURY HIGHLIGHTS

The hungry 30's
The films were great,
The start of the war.

The 'Roaring 40's'
Tacoma Bridge collapsed
The Second World War ended.

The funky 50's
TV came out,
Roger Bannister ran one mile in four minutes.

The swinging 60's
Washing machines were invented,
England won the World Cup.

The shiny 70's
First test tube baby,
Bay City Rollers sang with 'Tartan'.

John Stewart (11)
Balbardie Primary School

20TH CENTURY HIGHLIGHTS

Back in the depths of time
There was a war, it was a crime
Air raid sirens wailing
Battleships gone sailing
Back in the depths of time.

The war went on
For not so long
The damage caused
Could not be solved
Back in the depths of time.

Inventions galore
And so much more
Sputnik One
The space race begun
Back in the depths of time.

The World Cup was won
The space age re-run
The music
The fashion
Back in the depths of time.

Britain joined Europe
John Lennon shot
Margaret Thatcher
Boy, that's a lot!
Back . . . in the depths of time.

Scott Craig (11)
Balbardie Primary School

POEM OF THE CENTURY

The 30's started off so great
but then became so sad.
The war broke out in '39
and it was really bad.

The 40's was a happy time
because the war did end
But then guess what? Tacoma Bridge fell
oh, what happened then?

The fabulous 50's were so great
the satellite into space.
They had everything here
from exams to Elvis Presley.

The swinging sixties were a treat
and the fashion was fab.
England won the World Cup;
and 'Flower Power' began.

Now the 70's were just fine
when Britain joined Europe.
Mother Teresa won the Nobel Peace Prize
The 70's were keeping in time.

These are my only highlights
I am sure there are many more.
20th Century a happy time
Well, apart from the war!

Nicola Toms (11)
Balbardie Primary School

POEM OF THE CENTURY

The 30's were nice,
then came the war,
soon after that, guess
what came next?
A film 'Snow White'.

But guess what happened
next in the 40's?
Tacoma Bridge fell
to the ground.

Then came the 50's, oh yes!
The singing and dancing
of Presley. Then the
satellite into space.

Soon came the 60's
the miniskirt too.
To make it easy,
the washing machine too!

Then the 70's came
Mrs Thatcher first
British Prime Minister
and some great music
from John Lennon.

So there you go,
the 30's to the 70's
such great times in
every way.

Laura Burton (11)
Balbardie Primary School

20TH CENTURY HIGHLIGHTS

It was the 30's, the start of the war,
Bombs, bombs, bombs, bombs galore!
Children being evacuated
Away from their families forever more.
And there was Edward and Mrs Simpson
Edward gave up the throne for Mrs Simpson
He wasn't allowed to marry her because
                                    she was a divorcee.

Hooray! It's the 40's and the war's
Ended at last.
The Tacoma Bridge collapsed because
Of high winds. This was sad.

It was the time of song and dance
And Elvis Presley was 'king'!
And then Princess Elizabeth was crowned
And what a good Queen is she!

Then came rolling in, the 70's
When the first test tube baby was born
And she was a girl!
Margaret Thatcher was the first
British woman Prime Minister.
So there you have it!

The highlights of the 20th Century!

Amy Nisbet (11)
Balbardie Primary School

11

20TH CENTURY HIGHLIGHTS

The outbreak of the war
started in the 30's
people were hungry,
people were angry,
food was rationed
for there wasn't a lot.

In the 40's the war
continued and ended.
No more sirens
no more black-outs
the world was at peace.

In the fabulous 50's
Roger Bannister broke
the world record for
running a mile in
four minutes.
Elvis Presley made his
way to fame by
using his voice and singing.

The swinging 60's were
worn with pride, with
Miniskirts, washing machines
and the Beatles to listen to.
Neil Armstrong walked on
the moon and 'Flower Power'
was brought into fashion.

In the 70's Britain joined Europe
and John Lennon was shot.
There was the first test tube
baby and the Bay City Rollers . . .
in the super 70's.

These are the best of the highlights.

Chloe Parker (11)
Balbardie Primary School

20TH CENTURY HIGHLIGHTS POEM

Way, way back in 1939,
day-to-day life was going just fine
until . . . September!
Everything changed almost overnight
the sirens went off and people got a fright.
Food was rationed, signposts taken down
to make it hard for Hitler to find his way around.
June '45 and everything was done
the war was over and Britain had won!

In the 'Roaring 40's' the war had ended
no more bombs, no more sirens
Germans had stopped their firing.

In the 'Funky 50's' Elvis was famous
and TV was introduced.

In the 'Swinging 60's' Miniskirts came out
James Bond came back in action
and the girls began to shout.

In the 70's everyone liked 'Grease'
when it came out in the pictures on general release.

Samantha Allan (11)
Balbardie Primary School

20TH CENTURY HIGHLIGHTS

Hungry 30's

In the 1930's war began with Britain and Germany.
What a tragedy it was, people dying, people
sighing, wondering if it would ever happen again.
Disney's first film was released, 'Snow White
and the Seven Dwarfs', animals so kind and
the witch so evil.

Party 40's

In the 40's everybody was so pleased
because war was at an end.
'Let's have a party' one man said.
'No,' said a lady and went to bed.

Cool 50's

50's, 50's is so smart
With people dancing with their heart
This is when we started to dance,
To rock 'n' roll with a glance.
Roger Bannister ran one mile,
In four minutes it was a miracle
He didn't think he could do it
Yes he did, and we all knew it.

Short 60's

This is when we started to get short
With the low top and the skirts.
Everybody loved walking round
with all of these short clothes on.
Let's go rolling down the hill,
the 60's is when we started to get clean
bringing out the washing machine.

The late 70's

The video 'Grease' came out
Wit the gelled hair and wearing denim.
Britain joined Europe and were pleased,
So lets you know we will always be friends.

Heather Watson (11)
Balbardie Primary School

THE TWENTIETH CENTURY

1930's - Terrible War II begins,
evacuation comes into action.
Nylon is now in the fashion,
long dresses in fashion.

1940's - Anne Frank writes a diary.
Newborn child, Prince Charles.
Out comes the rationing book,
Princess Elizabeth marries Prince Philip.

1950's - Minis on sale,
New Cliff Richard becomes famous.
Coffee bars become popular.
Queen Elizabeth was crowned.

1960's - Twiggy became a model.
Beatles came into action.
Miniskirts are the fashion.
The swinging sixties.

1970's - Punks come into town.
Computers - the silicon chip came into use.
The twenty-first century is just about to begin.

Amy Houston (11)
Balbardie Primary School

TWENTIETH CENTURY

As the century takes its final bow
And waves its last farewell,
The long, sleek dress hangs left alone,
The tales that it could tell,
Of abdication, Olympic Games,
And Monopoly to sell.

The 'fighting forties' take control,
And bring the death toll high,
By bombs and guns and Spanish flu,
Yet as some people cry,
Life goes on, a prince is born,
Anne Frank's diary won't die.

Barbie, mini, forty years,
They've never had it so good!
New music, new Queen, new technology,
People smile as they should,
Teddy boys, full skirts, coffee bars,
The friendly fifties mood.

The sixties, round the corner roll,
Swinging into view,
Beatles rule, pop, Twiggy, catwalk,
With flowers green, red and blue.
Skirts get shorter . . . and shorter . . . and shorter
And their boots change their size too.

Punk rock hit the nation next,
With watches, the Walkman and all,
Let's remember the lessons of the past,
When the future comes to call.

Alice McNamara (11)
Balbardie Primary School

THE TWENTIETH CENTURY

Missing King,
But hold the bus!
Here comes a princess
Called Snow White
Who brings joy to all,
Helping them forget the war.

Brave Anne Frank -
Writing a diary in hiding.
Prince Charles was born
Food rationing came
And Princess Elizabeth
Married Prince Philip.

Newly-married Princess Elizabeth is crowned Queen
And Barbie is born into the world!
Cliff Richard sings his songs
Drive in your new Mini
Down to the coffee bar
And meet up with your friends.

Listen to the Beatles
And dance in your Miniskirts
See the latest fashions
On Twiggy in your newspaper
You're living in the
          Swinging Sixties'

It's the time of the 'punk rocker'
Margaret Thatcher is the first woman PM
The Walkman and the 'silicon chip',
                    jump into action.

Another busy decade!

Mhairi Borrowman (11)
Balbardie Primary School

TWENTIETH CENTURY POEM

In the 1930's Pluto was discovered
And also the war started
Which meant children had to be evacuated
To the country.
Also the VW Beetle came into use -
And 'Snow White' was released, what a happy time!

The forties saw Biro pens go on sale
And it also saw food rationing.
Our Queen married Prince Philip -
In 1947.
Gandhi was assassinated!
And in the same year Prince Charles was born -
Another busy time.

The Mini then came into use -
In 1959
Queen Elizabeth was crowned -
In 1953.
Cliff Richard is still hanging on
And there's new technology like -
The vacuum cleaner, the washing machine and much, much more.

This was known as the swinging sixties -
With Twiggy and the Beatles!
The Miniskirts were in fashion
At this time!

The fashion was punk rock at this time, the 1970's
Our PM was Margaret Thatcher
Silicon chips came out this time
Another busy time . . .

Stephen Wilkins (11)
Balbardie Primary School

18

TWENTIETH CENTURY

In the 1930's there was a big war,
Pluto was discovered and a lot more.
Nylon was invented,
Beetle came out.
This decade was weird without any doubt!

1940's, Edinburgh had a big parade.
A year before then the Biro was made.
Coal mines were nationalised,
NHS in Britain.
Anne's diary published five years
               from when it was written.

In the 1950's Elizabeth got crowned.
Cliff Richard's music was a popular sound.
Barbie was made up,
Coffee bars were opened
And Minis were invented somewhere near the end.

Swingin' 60's were the next decade,
That was when fashion was made.
Miniskirts, platform shoes,
And Beatles sometimes sang the blues.

1970's were full of rock,
Walkman was all the latest talk.
Mother Teresa,
Silicon chip,
1970's were really hip!

Now we're drawing to a close,
That's how the saying goes!

Tom McDonald (11)
Balbardie Primary School

THE TWENTIETH CENTURY

Some amazing events occurred
Edward abdicates!
He's gone to France - to meet his love,
Another king will take his place.

The 1940's - another decade,
Anne Frank and her diary,
The Battle of Britain,
Suddenly it ends - celebration!

The Mini and Barbie spell the 1950's
New and improved technology,
Washing machines, vacuum cleaners,
A new Queen.

A new fashion is here -
Miniskirts and these were mini!
The shorter, the better, they thought.
There is a new pop band
This band is it -
The Beatles!

There is another new fashion
This time it is punk!
Spiky hair, ripped jeans
This is a new fashion
We have a woman Prime Minister
Margaret Thatcher.

Lisa Pennycook (11)
Balbardie Primary School

THE TWENTIETH CENTURY

The twentieth century was an adventure
and that's where it all takes place.
In the 30's fashion was glamour and
the Empire State Building was the tallest in the place.
The VW Beetle was the craze!

The 40's had lots of happenings,
Prince Charles was born.
The first Biro pen was introduced by Laszlo Biró,
the war was still going on.
It lasted six years.

In the 50's, the Mini was invented,
along with the great Barbie doll!
Also, Queen Elizabeth was crowned
and coffee bars came out. *Yum!*

The swinging 60's!
The miniskirt and the big platforms!
Twiggy, the famous model, was out
modelling all the glamorous clothes.
The Beatles sang their hearts out.

In the 70's, people were turning into punks,
wearing leather jackets and leopard-skin trousers.
Then the wild, spiky hairstyles, which
they dyed all different colours.
A decade of colours and fun!

Lorena Brown (11)
Balbardie Primary School

THE 20TH CENTURY HIGHLIGHTS

The 1930's - a decade that saw
evacuation and abdication.
A planet discovered - little Pluto.
A car - a Beetle!
A game, still famous today -
Monopoly.

A diary - poor Anne Frank,
another tragic death.
The biro pen, still famous today -
a decade of change the 1940's.

The doll we all adore -
Barbie - 40 soon!
A car still famous today,
the Mini!

1960, the fashion decade.
The miniskirt!
A group still famous today -
The Beatles!

The 1970's were the years of the punk!
Margaret Thatcher was elected
as Prime Minister.
The silicon chip was introduced
and is still in use today!

Stephanie Tennant (11)
Balbardie Primary School

TWENTIETH CENTURY POEM

At the start of the century, poor Edward
abdicated for Wallis Simpson.
Then, there was the Olympics,
and then the war.
Children were evacuated
to places far away.

1940's - after the war,
Anne Frank - a young girl.
Her diary was published
about hiding through the war.
Biro pens were introduced -
but used mostly for ration books.

1950's sees a new queen.
Coffee bars to eat and drink in,
the Mini - the people's car,
Barbie, with her glossy hair!
New technology, TV's and vacuum cleaners.

1960's. Twiggy's on the scene.
but the Cold War goes on
inside people's heads.
A nice, new fashion,
miniskirts and all.
The Beatles come through your radio
at about 100 volts.

1970's, punk rockers rule the streets at night.
The first digital watches are worn,
no need for radios in the house,
just take a Walkman
outside with you.

Crawford Morgan (11)
Balbardie Primary School

THE TWENTIETH CENTURY

The twenty-first century soon.
Back in the 1930's long, sleek dresses were the fashion.
Edward abdicates.
Edward marries Mrs Wallis Simpson.
The VW Beetle is on the road.
War breaks out -
what a decade!

Food rationing,
the Olympics were in London,
Prince Charles was born,
The Diary of Anne Frank was published.
The war is over - the country celebrates.

The Mini was on the road,
everyone was at coffee bars,
Elizabeth was crowned as queen.
Cliff Richard jumped into the charts.
A decade of change.

It's the swinging 60's,
The Beatles were the pop group.
Miniskirts were the fashion,
every girl wanted to be like Twiggy.
A swinging decade.

Punks were here, they were the fashion.
Margaret Thatcher was the first woman Prime Minister.
The Walkman came out -
a changing time.

Laura Stephen (11)
Balbardie Primary School

THE TWENTIETH CENTURY

1930's - Pluto discovered.
A great four medal win
In the Berlin Olympics for Jesse Owens.
Abdication! Edward marries Mrs Simpson.
Volkswagen Beetle -
storms in and hits the road - the people's car!

Olympics hit again, but in London.
Queen finds love,
marries Prince Philip.
Biro pen steps in -
takes over and becomes
'the' pen to write with.

The 1950's. Barbie comes to town
and is still in action.
Queen Elizabeth,
crowned 1953.
A small car - The Mini,
comes in 1959 - the car to be in!

Twiggy, the model - the lady
of the swinging sixties.
Miniskirts - the best fashion for ladies.
Beatles break out
on the radio.

The big punk rock
in the 70's.
Margaret Thatcher - the
first woman Prime Minister.
The Walkman bursts out for the young ones!

William Mitchell (11)
Balbardie Primary School

TWENTIETH CENTURY WORLD

The twentieth century fashions were incredible.
Pluto was discovered at the same time!
Monopoly was the best-selling game ever
and is still bought today!

The 1940's - the first biro was invented.
Princess Elizabeth married Prince Philip too.
New materials were discovered, new fashions too.
The atomic bomb was tested in 1945. Bang!

The 1950's - the first portable radio, everyone's dream.
Elvis Presley in 1954 sang all the new songs!
The Mini car! Barbie, a little girl's dream come true,
she was made for me and you in the 1950's.

Twiggy - what a model in the swinging sixties.
The miniskirt for loads of fun, James Bond -
the film, and then the first moon walk in July 1969.

In 1970, the punk generation - red and green hair.
The great film 'Jaws' was released.
In 1970, the first personal stereo and of course, the camcorder!
The twentieth century is about to end.
Welcome to the twenty-first century!

Michael Buntin (11)
Balbardie Primary School

CELEBRATIONS

One day it was my birthday,
It made me thirsty.
It was so great,
That I was about to break.
It was on a Thursday.

Christmas is so great,
That it's as good as steak.
There're lots of presents,
But none for peasants
I hope you're not too late.

Kevin Swankie (10)
Balbardie Primary School

TWENTIETH CENTURY

The twentieth century, oh how grand.
There are some bits that aren't so nice though,
like the war, the violence, the evacuation too.
Boy, you're lucky it wasn't you.
Pluto was discovered, oh what a sight.
You could only see it in the darkness of night.

In the 1940's, Anne Frank's Diary. The Biro pen is born.
The Queen marries Prince Philip and Prince Charles is born.
The Olympics are in London and foods are rationed.

Then the 1950's come into view. Barbie's born.
Cliff Richard is singing too.
The Mini drives along the street, to have one was a treat.
Queen Elizabeth crowned in 1953, oh how I wish it was me.

Then the 1960's hop along, let's listen to a Beatles song.
Then miniskirts come into fashion and everyone is jumping
and thumping in high boots.

The 1970's come into place, that's when punk rock
stars were swinging and grooving.
The silicon chip is being produced. Yeah, video games
come in to use.

Leona Rodden (11)
Balbardie Primary School

THE TWENTIETH CENTURY

The 1930's dawn,
children enjoy 'Snow White', Monopoly.
The war begins -
children don't enjoy the evacuation.

Poor Anne Frank -
the writer of the diary.
The war is over!
Princess Elizabeth marries -
the country celebrates.

Driving in comes the Mini,
Barbie bursts into action,
Cliff Richard singing on the radio.
No more dirty houses -
the new vacuum cleaner is the answer.

The swinging sixties,
the crowd dance to The Beatles.
The miniskirt,
high, knee-length boots.
Fashion!

Punk rockers - fashion.
Margaret Thatcher - the new power.
Looking forward to the new century,
what changes will we see?

Tracey Muirhead (11)
Balbardie Primary School

THE TWENTIETH CENTURY

The 1930's are here! Abdication, fashion, war, Pluto,
Empire State Building.
Pluto is the ninth planet in the solar system.
It was discovered by Clyde Tombaugh.
Here comes the Barbie Doll!
It's here to stay - forty years old!

Here is the 40's, Prince Charles is born.
Anne Frank's Diary is published.
The Princess marries her Prince,
the Olympic Games were held in London.

Here comes the 50's!
The coffee bars will all the people,
meeting and listening to music.
Queen crowned!

Here comes the 1960's.
Twiggy, the supermodel, up and down the catwalk.
Here comes the miniskirt up to your thighs.
The Beatles singing - everybody loved them in the 60's.

Here come the 70's - the punk look,
everybody in net tights with holes.
Margaret Thatcher, the first woman Prime Minister.
Here comes the silicon chip to put inside your computer!

Megan Bain (11)
Balbardie Primary School

THE TWENTIETH CENTURY

Twentieth century is about to close.
We start to think about the millennium.
Everybody's celebrating.
New technology is brought out.
The war began
in the 1930's.
Everyone buying the Biro pen.
The Queen married Prince Philip.
Hoover that makes cleaning easier came out.

Coffee bars are now open.
Everybody is buying Barbie.
New Mini car has come out.
Twiggy, the new model
up on the stage.
Rock music,
young people love the sound.

Natasha MacKay (11)
Balbardie Primary School

MILLENNIUM

M illennium is coming near,
I t is a new millennium.
L ights flashing all night long,
L ots of parties going on.
E veryone is partying,
N ew Year's celebrations will last all night.
N ot an experience to forget,
I nto a new millennium we go.
U nder the deep blue sky fireworks going off, they fly.
M ay everyone enjoy the fun still to come.

Robert Murray (10)
Balbardie Primary School

IT WILL BE A GREAT YEAR

M illennium is a special year,
I t is filled with enjoyment and cheer.
L aughing and parties are so much fun,
L eisure and games for everyone.
E njoying food, dancing to music,
N oisy games don't be sad if you lose it!
N ow is the time to prepare our celebrations
I t's lots of fun.
U nusual lights and fireworks in the sky.
M illennium will be a great year celebrated
    with Champagne and beer.

Jenna Stewart (10)
Balbardie Primary School

BIG PARTY

M illennium is coming near,
I t will be a new era.
L ights flashing all night,
L ovely sights all around.
E njoying music,
N ew Year is on its way.
N ow we will prepare our celebrations,
I nteresting things will happen.
U nder the sky fireworks will explode up in the air.
M ore parties for the millennium.

Steven Troup (10)
Balbardie Primary School

WORLD PARTY

C enturies are going on,
E earth will be partying all through the night.
L ots of people will be singing Auld Lang Syne,
E veryone is going to be there,
B est it's ever been!
R ocking parties everywhere,
A nd festivals with fireworks.
T his is the millennium!
I t's the best we've ever seen.
O n and on through '99 and,
N ow it's the millennium!

Kay Russell (10)
Balbardie Primary School

FUTURE

M agical new future
I mpressive ideas
L ateral thinking
L ess poverty
E xciting possibilities
N ew millennium
N ew ideas
I ntergalactic excitement
U nfolding the future
M illennium!

Marshall Inglis (11)
Balbardie Primary School

WHEN THE CLOCK STRIKES 12 WE WILL CELEBRATE

C elebrations will be held when the clock strikes 12,
E verybody will have a party to welcome in the year 2000.
L ots of computers will crash!
E dinburgh will hold a huge street party with drink and fireworks.
B rand new millennium will arrive.
R ight until Big Ben rings,
A nyone can get ready to celebrate.
T ime will go fast until the millennium,
I t will be fun for everyone.
O n January 1st 2000 we will party like animals,
N ight-time will come but we will still party on.

Graeme Shaw (10)
Balbardie Primary School

THE YEAR 2000

M aybe you'll have parties and discos at the millennium
I n streets they'll be partying.
L ots of people will be there,
L et everyone have a good time this year.
E vents might come to Bathgate,
N ew Year is special but not as special as this one.
N ow it's time to celebrate in style.
I n London there's a Millennium Dome being built,
U nbelievable things are happening.
M y family are going to have a great time!

Stephanie Size (10)
Balbardie Primary School

CELEBRATIONS

C elebrations are very, very fun.
E very year people celebrate for the New Year.
L ovely time, people are singing and dancing,
E very time people think of it
B right lights shining all night long.
R ed and blue lights shining.
A ll the people talking non-stop.
T he town all celebrates.
I love the music
O n the lights, red and blue.
N obody wants to go to bed.

Stephen McNab (10)
Balbardie Primary School

THE MILLENNIUM

M illions of people come from all around to celebrate.
I n the evening everyone will party after midnight.
L ove it or not the noise will be deafening.
L eap into the millennium.
E veryone gathers around to see the fireworks,
N o one will miss the celebrations.
N ight to remember
I t will be a great event
U nbelievable noise will be coming from the crowd.
M illennium comes once every thousand years.

Christopher Houston (10)
Balbardie Primary School

Move Into The Future

M agical, marvellous, merry new future,
I nstruments play to celebrate the new century.
L aughing out loud with delight and the happiness,
L ots of dancing and singing all around the streets,
E verlasting fun 'til night comes.
N ew century comes bringing hope and joy,
N obody will miss the fun at the millennium.
I nto a new era we move once again,
U nbelievable sights and sounds.
M ay everyone enjoy the fun times still to come.

Caroline Walker (10)
Balbardie Primary School

The Millennium

M illennium means the year 2000,
I am having a street party to celebrate the millennium.
L ots of other people are having a street party,
L ots of laughter and excitement,
E verybody will be invited,
N obody will be left out,
N obody will miss the celebrations.
I might not see the Millennium Dome,
U p in the sky there will be fireworks.
M y street will certainly enjoy the millennium.

Marie Lawton (10)
Balbardie Primary School

YEAR 2000

C elebrate the year 2000,
E veryone is making plans for parties,
L ovely food and drinks,
E veryone enjoys,
B rilliant games,
R eady to have a good time,
A t 7 o'clock my party's just ready,
T ime to party on,
I 'm ready to have a blast,
O n New Year's Eve
N ever to be forgotten.

Laura Rosie (10)
Balbardie Primary School

MILLENNIUM 2000

M illennium is a period of 1000 years,
I t's a completely new era about to begin,
L ots of parties everywhere,
L ots of things to prepare,
E veryone is getting ready,
N earer and nearer the millennium comes,
N ow we need to prepare,
I t's getting really exciting,
U pon knowing that it's time,
M illennium 2000.

Michael Ward (10)
Balbardie Primary School

CELEBRATIONS!

C elebrations are loads of fun,
E verybody loves them.
L ots of fun and games,
E njoy the wonderful moments.
B ouncing up and down, eating sticky puddings
R ound and round you go
A re you having a good time?
T urning, bouncing, round and round making funny faces
I t's nearly all over
O h no! Just a few more minutes,
N ow don't be sad
S tay right there! *Dong!* It's all over.

Megan Walker (10)
Balbardie Primary School

MILLENNIUM FUN

M idnight is the time to start celebrating.
I nto a new millennium.
L ots of parties and special events,
L ovely times ahead.
E veryone is enjoying
N on-stop fun.
N ice things for us all,
I nto a new era,
U tter happiness,
M illennium fun!

Peter Taylor (10)
Balbardie Primary School

IT'S A TIME TO CHEER

M illennium is coming up, it's getting very near,
I t's a time to celebrate,
L eaving homes, going to shops,
L ots of events getting near,
E veryone is preparing for the millennium,
N o one should be in a mood,
N ot at this special time,
I n and out the people will run about having fun,
U pon knowing that it's near, everyone give a great big cheer.
M illennium is coming near, it's time for a cheer!

Kyle Gibson (10)
Balbardie Primary School

NEW THINGS WILL COME

M illennium starts in the year 2000,
I t lasts for 1000 years.
L eaving the 20th century,
L iving the future will be fun.
E ntering a new life,
N ew things will come,
N ew experiences for young and old,
I t will be so exciting.
U naware of what will happen,
M illennium!

Jamie J Firth (10)
Balbardie Primary School

MILLENNIUM

M illennium Bug! A disaster waiting to happen.
I t will all disappear, all electricity, it will just flow and go.
L et us have a party, let whooshing fireworks fly!
L et magical stars float into the sky!
E ven when you have a party, nothing ever dawns.
N o lights, no warmth, no water sprinkling the lawns.
N ot even music blaring loud or computers that never vowed.
I love having parties, I know everyone does.
U unknown by some about this Millennium Bug.
M illennium Bug! Millennium Bug!

Lauren Sharkey (9)
Balbardie Primary School

MY MILLENNIUM

M illennium means a thousand years,
I am very fortunate to live to see the millennium
L et alone the new century.
L et's have a party or festival at the millennium.
E verybody is cheerful and excited at the millennium,
N ew year, new century, new millennium.
N ew and exciting times.
I 'm happy all the same,
U ntil the millennium ends,
M y millennium means a lot to me.

Margaret Binnie (10)
Balbardie Primary School

MILLENNIUM

M illennium excitement has gripped us,
I mportant things are happening at the millennium,
L ots of money will be spent.
L ovely parties and discos to attend,
E veryone will have a great time.
N ow we'll be entering a new millennium
N ot everyone will be as lucky as we are.
I nteresting times for us,
U ndo all the bad things we have done.
M illennium will be great!

Morven Hamilton (10)
Balbardie Primary School

THE YEAR 2000

M illennium is a period of one thousand years.
I am having a party,
L ots of people coming,
L ots of fun and laughter.
E veryone will light fireworks.
N ew Year's festival.
N ew experiences for young and old,
I will see the Millennium Dome.
U naware of what will happen next,
M y party will never end.

Angela McKay (10)
Balbardie Primary School

MILLENNIUM

M any people will be celebrating the millennium,
I t will be great.
L et's all enjoy the millennium,
L et's celebrate the start of a new era.
E njoy all the parties,
N o one should miss out on the celebrations.
N ew experiences for us all,
I nto the sky fly the fireworks.
U p in high buildings people watch everyone celebrating
   the new millennium.
M illennium fever!

Scott Brown (11)
Balbardie Primary School

MILLENNIUM

M y family are having a dressing-up party,
I t's going to be very good.
L et's find a good suit,
L et's order the food.
E veryone's going to be there.
N othing will stop us getting ready.
N uts, crisps and lots of juice,
I t'll be a great success,
U nlikely to go wrong.
M illennium is nearly here.

Gary Clark (10)
Balbardie Primary School

MILLENNIUM

M oving to a brand new year, Oh! How exciting
I t's special this time, it's coming near.
L aughter at twelve, dancing too
L et's take a break, I'm tired through.
E nough's enough, I am far too sleepy
N ew millennium party ends
N ow I'm too tired to move an inch
I t's four in the morning, that's why, that's why
U ntil now I never took the time to realise
M illenniums only come every thousand years.

Fiona Wood (10)
Balbardie Primary School

LOOK INTO THE FUTURE

M illennium is a special year,
I t's the start of year 2000.
L ights are flashing all night long,
L ots of fun for everyone.
E ntertainment for a while,
N ight-time dancing in the Dome.
N ot a time that we will forget,
I n a minute we will hear the bells of Big Ben.
U nderneath the Millennium Dome,
M ost people are celebrating and ready to cheer.

Lisa Cairns (10)
Balbardie Primary School

THE SOLAR SYSTEM

T o space we go.
H ere I come space.
E arth is a big planet in space.

S olar System has nine planets.
O ff to space we go.
L ight in the Solar System
A round Mars.
R ed is the colour of Mars.

S tars are nice,
Y ellow stars are bright.
S tars are bright and colourful.
T he sun is a big star.
E ach star pattern has its own name.
M ission accomplished.

Alan Peace (9)
Balbardie Primary School

BIRTHDAYS

My birthday is on the 13th of July,
You'd think it would be sooner.

Bring lots of presents and people,
I would like Bart Simpson on my birthday cake.
Remember it's my birthday,
The family will be celebrating.
'Happy birthday,' everybody shouts,
Do you like birthdays?
A time of your life,
You're coming to my birthday.

Christopher Mollon (10)
Balbardie Primary School

MILLENNIUM TWO THOUSAND

M illions of people will come.
I n the streets they will sing.
L ike little birds in winter,
L ittle drops of rain.
E verybody will enjoy it,
N ew Year is an hour away.
N ew Year's Day for the year two thousand.
I n the world is glee and happiness.
U p on the stars and planets
M illennium is drawing near.

T he world will sing and dance.
W hat will happen when it is all over?
O pen the door and go to sleep.

T he bell did ring and the traffic did stop.
H appy New Year everybody shouts.
O pen the door for the year two thousand.
U nder and to the moon and back.
S and will shift off the deserts
A nd grass will turn greener than ever.
N ever have I seen a millennium
D ive into the future for it is very soon.

Johnathan MacLeod (11)
Balbardie Primary School

CELEBRATION!

Celebration is time to fiddle,
There is no time to read a riddle.
Ready to whistle and have fun,
And there is time to eat a chocolate bun.

Time to see the bells on television,
Run and get the glasses from the kitchen.
Have red wine on top of some pine;
And do a little dance in a line.

Kylie Ebbs (10)
Balbardie Primary School

READY FOR TAKE OFF

The suits are on
So let's be gone (10)
I really don't know what to do
I know I will really miss you (9)
We have to check the crew
And we are all new (8)
I think we could all do
With help from you (7)
Do you think I will make it
I am in and sitting (6)
I will live on the moon
And I will dance till noon (5)
I feel really silly
Who is that boy Billy? (4)
But we are all very sore (3)
You think I am a mean person
But I am very, very sweet (2)
You like me now
I think you are nice (1)
Lift Off!

Victoria Wilson (9)
Balbardie Primary School

A HAUNTED HOUSE

Scary black, spiders
Making a spider web.
Slimy, green, monsters
Scaring people that pass.
Hooting grey owls
Wake me from my sleep.

Ghosts are speaking
It is really freaking.
Bats are covered in goo
Freaky monsters are spooky too.
Slimy gunge
Dripping all the time.

The haunted house looks spooky
It really is.
It has crooked vines
And the wallpaper is covered in lines.
Doors are creaking
It is the haunted house.

Lyle Donald Robert Cameron (9)
Balbardie Primary School

CELEBRATION (MY BIRTHDAY)

I awoke that morning and turned on the light,
to see all my presents shiny and bright.
Then my uncle came through and gave me a ball,
boy he is tall, although I am very small.
That evening as I turned off the light,
I murmured to myself my birthday this year has been alright.

Amy Craise (10)
Balbardie Primary School

THE SOLAR SYSTEM

T o space we go.
H eading to Saturn.
E arth is getting left behind.

S aturn has bright rings orbiting the sun.
O ff to Jupiter we go
L ovely stripes Jupiter has.
A rocket zooming in the air.
R ings around Saturn sparkling.

S un is very bright.
Y ellow is Venus with no rings.
S aturn is all different colours
T o infinity and beyond.
E veryone is diving on Pluto
M ight visit you again.

Gillian Thomson (9)
Balbardie Primary School

MILLENNIUM

M illennium is 1000 years
I t's time to celebrate.
L ittle boys and little girls
L ots of fun for them.
E xcitement flying through the air
N ow it's time to party.
N oisy fireworks shoot through the air
I mmense pop groups playing music.
U nbelievable to be here
M illennium!

Gavin Szweblik (10)
Balbardie Primary School

THE SOLAR SYSTEM

T o the moon we go.
H ere we are floating in the air.
E arth is behind.

S un is nearby.
O ff we go away to the moon.
L ots of planets nearby.
A re you sure that you can walk on the moon?
R ed Mars goes by.

S un is next to Mercury.
Y es, we're there
S tanding on the moon.
T oday we are coming back from the moon to
E arth.
M ercury is next to the sun.

Stacey Sutherland (9)
Balbardie Primary School

MILLENNIUM

M illennium
I t must be fun
L ittle boys
L ittle girls
E veryone's having a party
N o one is being bad
N oisy crackling from sparkling fireworks
I 'm very glad
U unbelievable sights
M illennium!

Steven Strachan (10)
Balbardie Primary School

THE SOLAR SYSTEM

T o space we go. Bye.
H ere we go.
E arth is far behind.

S aturn is very colourful
O ribiting the sun.
L ike a ball of fire.
A rocket is floating through space.
R ed is the colour of Mars.

S o the Earth is bright as light
Y ou're to the moon.
S miles of the people
T he nice planets.
E verything looks pretty.
M aybe we'll be back.

Megan Bell (8)
Balbardie Primary School

MILLENNIUM

Soaring high into the sky,
The rocket goes I don't know why.
It's coming near the turning of a thousand years.
The day is gone
And the next new era dawns.
The lights go out without a shout
And I'm as pleased as punch.
I've got a hunch,
That the new millennium is here!

Dean Edwards Mollon (10)
Balbardie Primary School

THE SOLAR SYSTEM

T he sun is hot and yellow.
H ow the planets dwell
E ven though the sun is hot, there I still want to go.

S aturn is pretty with quite a few moons
O h how nice are Saturn's rings
L ots of stars around it
A nd also the lovely colours all over it
R ound and round the sun it goes.

S pace is brill, space is fab
Y elling volumes zero.
S pace is brill, space is fab
T rying to get to Mars
E arth is left behind
M aybe I'll get there soon.

Heather Hopkins (8)
Balbardie Primary School

MILLENNIUM

M illennium is a thousand years,
I t must be so much fun.
L ittle boys running about the street
L oving every bit.
E xcitement in the air, excitement everywhere.
N oisy people screaming and shouting.
N oisy cannons blasting.
I know that people love fireworks.
U nbelievable sights.
M illennium.

Lee Pringle (10)
Balbardie Primary School

THE SOLAR SYSTEM

T he Solar System is very pretty
H ere we come to get you
E arth is very small.

S un is a ball of fire
O ver the moon and far away.
L ittle things are floating about.
A h! The stars are so pretty.
R ed is the colour of pretty Mars.

S aturn is a big planet
Y ou are going to Neptune
S eeing Uranus is great
T hey are all very pretty
E ven Pluto is nice
M any planets are pretty.

Jennifer Smillie (9)
Balbardie Primary School

MILLENNIUM

M illennium Bug
I   s coming soon.
L ots of fireworks
L ight as the moon.
E veryone's excited,
N obody crying,
N obody sad.
I   am not angry, I am glad.
U nbelievable to be here,
M illenniums don't come every year!

Janine Dunn (10)
Balbardie Primary School

THE SOLAR SYSTEM

T hree, two, one, blast off.
H ot Mercury (I'm not touching that)
E arth is very far behind us.

S aturn is excellent.
O ff we go to Pluto because it's near . . . *Brrr!* That's freezing.
L ots of stars in the Solar System.
A liens evaporating astronauts.
R ay guns . . . *Aarrgh!*

S o then let's go to Venus
Y ellow it is, next to, *Ouch,* I told you it was hot.'
S et the rocket on faster, the sun is hotter.
T o Earth I tell you or we're going to explode.
E h, hello do it I tell you.
M y word I'm glad that's over.

Sean Ferguson (9)
Balbardie Primary School

MILLENNIUM

M agical millennium
I n the kingdom
L ots of parties
L ots of excited people.
E verybody's happy waiting for the bells.
N obody is sad
N obody's crying, nobody's bad.
I n their house safe and glad
U nbelievable site - the Millennium Dome
M illennium will be fun!

Vicki Brown (10)
Balbardie Primary School

THE SOLAR SYSTEM

T he rocket goes into space.
H ere we are in space.
E verything is moving round.

S kip, run, jump, can't walk on the Moon.
O rbit the sun, that's the planets.
L arge ball of fire glowing. Can you guess? Yes it's the Sun.
A re you sure you would like to hear some more.
R ush, rush, rush, going round the Sun.

S aturn's rings are so beautiful.
Y ou have to be brave in space.
S o quiet in space.
T wo people are scared
E arth is so small.
M y trip was really exciting. I would like to go back.

Aimee Ovens (9)
Balbardie Primary School

MILLENNIUM

M illennium is fun and groovy bells ring to let it in.
I t's coming to get the computers, it's the Millennium Bug.
L et's have parties, let's have fun. People dancing, people singing.
L et all the bells ring, let the party begin.
E veryone singing with glee, dancing and shouting with me.
N ow it's fireworks, colours in the dark-black sky.
N ow watch them die into the sky.
I t's the Millennium Bug, watch out here it comes.
U ntil the day comes I'll have fun.
M illennium is the greatest thing on Earth. It won't be long
before it's gone.

Scott Campbell (10)
Balbardie Primary School

THE SOLAR SYSTEM

T o Mars I go
H op into the spaceship
E ek! Away we go.

S unny over here.
O h I can see Mars
L ovely colour it is
A nd we've missed Mars
R ight, turn back.

S aturn is in sight.
Y es we are back on track.
S lowly, slowly we don't want to crash.
T hump we've landed
E ven here it's hot
M ission success, over and out.

Jemma Black (9)
Balbardie Primary School

CELEBRATION!

It's the celebration of the year,
The people in the streets will cheer.
Fireworks spray into the sky,
Parties begin and streamers fly.

The bells will soon start to ring,
People will do the highland fling.
The excited people jump and cheer,
For the biggest celebration of the year!

Lauren Bradley (9)
Balbardie Primary School

THE SOLAR SYSTEM

T o infinity and beyond
H ere we go up to the moon
E arth is a big planet

S aturn is the second biggest planet
O ff we go up to space
L ots of stars up in the sky
A re there lots of planets in the sky
R ed Mars goes round and round

S aturn is the sixth planet from the sun
Y es we are going to the moon
S aturn is a very big planet
T omorrow we are going home
E arth is a big planet
M ercury is next to the sun.

Lee Houston (10)
Balbardie Primary School

MILLENNIUM

M idnight, the millennium strikes.
I think some people would like to fly kites.
L arge, large crowds look to the sky.
L arge, large crowds say, 'My, oh my!'
E veryone is thrilled.
N obody should be killed this year.
N ot a person not having fun.
I hope everyone enjoys themselves.
U p to the fridge and have a bun.
M illennium, millennium have fun on the millennium.

Mhairi Tennant (9)
Balbardie Primary School

THE SOLAR SYSTEM

T oday is the day
H e flies to the moon
E veryone was cheering as we blasted off.

S o I can't go back.
O ff to the moon
L eaving Earth behind
A re we there? No we're not
R ace towards the moon.

S ometimes I'm scared
Y es! We're there
S tanding on the moon
T oday is the day we're coming back to
E arth
M aybe I will come again.

Lyndsay Reid (9)
Balbardie Primary School

MILLENNIUM

M en and women have lived for thousands of years.
I celebrate outside.
L ots of people out and about.
L ots of streamers everywhere.
E xciting fireworks light up the sky.
N ow it's time to party.
N ew millennium.
I t's time to go to a party.
U ntil the next millennium is here.
M idnight, we party all through the night.

Gerard Stryker (10)
Balbardie Primary School

THE SOLAR SYSTEM

T o space we go
H eading to Mars
E arth is a little planet

S un is like a fireball
O ver Mars we go
L ike red-hot ashes
A man orbiting Pluto
R ound and round.

S tars
Y ellow is the colour of Venus
S aturn is a very big planet
T o infinity
E verything is floating
M ission completed.

Dean Buntin (9)
Balbardie Primary School

MILLENNIUM

M illennium, millennium
I t's a celebration
L et's have a party
L et's celebrate the creation
E verything lit up
N everending parties
N ew 1000 years
I n with millions of cheers
U p in the sky rockets fly
M any people stay up all night.

Ben Robertson (10)
Balbardie Primary School

HAPPINESS AND SADNESS

Happiness is . . .
Swimming in the cool sparkling water.
Surfing in the warm foaming waves.
Watching the red roses bloom.
Playing in the soft warm water.
Drawing cartoon pictures in my room.
Watching the Simpsons on TV.
Scoring a hat-trick and everyone cheering.
Practising at tricks on my blades.

Sadness is . . .
My friend falling out with me.
When my gran died.
Having to play on my own.
When I hurt myself.
My friends shouting at me.

But most of the time I am happy.

Victoria Brown (9)
Balbardie Primary School

MILLENNIUM

The Millennium Bug thought he was smug sitting on a microchip.
Fireworks flying into the sky,
Looping the loop, swirling, exploding then dying so high.
Get ready to party,
Have some fun,
Because the food will be yum, yum, yum.
A celebration of fun and laughter.

Stuart Malloy (9)
Balbardie Primary School

DISASTER AT LIFT OFF

Spaceship at the ready
Inside it's nice and tidy (10)

When I'm lying in bed
It feels like everything else is dead (9)

People in the space hut like me
Think we'll miss our families (8)

We are all praying that we'll soon
Be on the pure-white moon (7)

Last check to see if we're ready
And if everyone has got their teddy (6)

Up on deck the satellite got pecked
And half of the ship fell off (5)

We all began to panic
The captain had gone manic (4)

The countdown would have to stop
Or the spaceship would go pop (3)

The mission was aborted and
Everything was sorted (2)

We all went home to our mums and dads
Took off our coats and unpacked our bags (1)

In the end we didn't go because of that stupid crow.

Lee Melrose (9)
Balbardie Primary School

LIFT OFF . . .

'Is everything ready?' the pilot shouts
Up in space nobody can grouch.
Ten

With a *whoosh! Zoom! Zap! Bang!*
We hear the engines start to clang
Nine

Thinking about the aliens I might find
I might take something back, I hope they don't mind.
Eight

Is all the equipment ready? Check.
Where's all the food? It's up on deck!
Seven

I wonder where we're going, maybe to the moon
all I really wish is we'll be there soon!
Six

Oh! I feel so hot in here
I wish a freezer would appear.
Five

I'm not looking forward to the food out of a tube
I wish I could have some hot tomato soup.
Four

I wonder if the stars look fine
I hope it's not a waste of time.
Three

I wish we were ready to go
I'll miss the sound of my dog Po!
Two

Excitement, fear mixed together
I'll never feel the same forever
One

Blast Off!

Jamie Nelson (9)
Balbardie Primary School

THE SNOWMAN

There once was a snowman
Who lived on his own
He had one special friend
Her name was Joan.

Joan liked everything
Spick and span
But never seemed to
Lend a hand.

John had to do all the work,
While Joan sat back and watched.
Every day got worse and worse,
Until his back did crack.

John became very weak
And couldn't do the work.
So in the end she didn't have a choice
She did it herself.

Polly Hazel Craig (9)
Balbardie Primary School

EARTH DAY

There once was a spaceman called Tim
Who lived in a old biscuit tin
He danced on the moon
Ate dust from a spoon
And became weak and frustrated and thin.

There once was a lady called Mars
Who lived on millions of stars
She loved the stars
She liked Earth and Mars
But the best one was Saturn.

Abigail McConnell (9)
Balbardie Primary School

EARTH DAY

There once was a spaceman called Tim
Who lived in a old biscuit tin
He danced on the moon
Ate dust from a spoon
And became weak and frustrated and thin.

There once was a lady called Mars
Who went to see the stars
Round the block
And ran into an alien car.

Steven Halloren (9)
Balbardie Primary School

WINDY DAY

Out and about in the countryside,
Grass bending like a man before a king.
The breeze making my hair stick up like a porcupine's spikes.
People walking like they are in slow motion.
The noise was oh so deafening in my little ears.
The leaves rolling about like little miniature balls.
Buckets crashing and rolling down the hill.
Suddenly the wind stopped
It was oh so still.
I thought for a moment the world was at an end.
The peacefulness didn't last long
The wind then came up again
I then knew that the world was not at an end.

Gemma Wright (9)
Balbardie Primary School

THE FRIEND

'What a trip!
We're on the Planet *Zork*!'
'Planet Stork?'
'No *Zork*!'
'Get the crew!'
'Get the zoo?'
'No crew!'
Rahhh!
'Ah! Get the car.
Aliens! What next?'
Bang!
'Oh no! The ship's broken down.'

Callum McLean (9)
Balbardie Primary School

THE SOLAR SYSTEM

T o space we go
H eading to the galaxy
E arth is far away

S un shining like a ball
O rbiting the sun
L oading off to Mars
A liens running round Saturn
R ed stars going by

S tars are shining bright
Y ippee I am at the moon
S aturn is colourful
T empted to go to Jupiter
E verything floating around
M ercury is very hot.

Gregor Allan (9)
Balbardie Primary School

ANTS

Ants are strong.
Ants are fast.
Ants are little.
Ants are black or red.
Ants go everywhere.
I'm not very keen on ants!
Ants are small.
Ants are slimy.
Ants are horrible.
Ants are poisonous.

Christopher Malloy (7)
Balbardie Primary School

ANOTHER WORLD

Mission Control, we have landed.
We can't believe it, it's enchanted.
Sparks are flying through the air
Asteroids are everywhere.

The planet getting closer all the time
Mobius looks covered in sticky slime.
I've seen an alien, what a shock!
The alien looks like a spotty sock.

The stench of it was killing.
Then the alien starting singing.
The words it sang were like this,
'Blip, blop, blogen, bliss!'

I decided to run back to my ship
The alien gave me one last nip.
I took off in my space rocket
I took a look at my fuel socket.

We're running very low on fuel
And I'm getting extremely cool.
The planet now is a grain of sand,
Mission Control we're about to land.

Oh no! Oh no!
We're about to crash
Help us, Mission Control!
Czete ! Czete! Bash!

Samuel James Thomson (9)
Balbardie Primary School

A STRANGE PLANET

5, 4, 3, 2, 1 blast off.
Mission Control, we're off to tin planet.
Ah! We've just hit a high flying gannet.
Now we're steady and ready to go.

We have now landed successfully
The planet is a shiny metal colour.
It's surprisingly bright.

Wow! A metallic kingdom
Let's check it out at random.
This place is deserted
Let's have fun.

Let's play that pinball machine.
I'm going to play sliding with Joe.
Now it's time to go home, *boo, hoo!*
Will we tell the humans about this?
No they'll never believe us!

Darren Dalrymple (9)
Balbardie Primary School

FORKED LIGHTNING

Forked lightning is frightening.
It lights in the night.
You might see it light in the night.
The lightning comes out in the cold, dark night.
You might hear the thunder with the lightning too.
And it could rain.

Siobhan Pirrie (7)
Balbardie Primary School

WINTER

Look at the snow all glossy and white
The frost is sparkling in the sunlight.
The snow is so white
And the sun is so bright.

The pond is so frosty
And the mud is so slushy.
Icicles are so sharp
As sharp as knives.

Snowmen are built every year
Built in people's back gardens.
Everyone dancing out on the street
With their wellies on their feet.

Alan Stewart (9)
Balbardie Primary School

HAPPINESS . . .

Happiness is . . .
A long bath in bubbly water
Taking the dog out for a run
Getting away from the noise in class
Going on holiday
Sunbathing on the beach
Playing volleyball on the beach

Sadness is . . .
Someone dying
Getting bullied
When someone pulls my hair
Getting lots of homework.

Erin Nisbet (9)
Balbardie Primary School

SPACEMAN

Last night I saw a spaceman
He was a very chubby man.
You'll never guess what his spaceship was
A large frying pan!

Next morning he flew into my class
And knocked my teacher out!
We were all very happy
And gave a loud shout!

He landed in the cupboard
As he flew into my house.
he climbed on to the drawing board
And killed my pet mouse!

At teatime
he flew into the room.
He crashed into a china pot,
Crash! Bang! Boom!

He came to me
And said goodbye.
Off he went
His spaceship disappeared into the sky.

Paul Stuart Hadden (9)
Balbardie Primary School

ANT

Ant, you are fast, speedy, quick to move!
Ant, you are strong and tough.
Ant, you munch and you bite.
Ant, you are tiny and you are red.

Michelle Addison (7)
Balbardie Primary School

HAPPINESS AND SADNESS

Happiness is . . .
Going to the movies and buying popcorn.
Swimming in the cool salty sea water.
Watching Eastenders on TV.
Going on a bike ride at Beecraigs.
Playing badminton with my friends.
Listening to my favourite CD.

Sadness is . . .
When I fall and scrape my knee.
When I am ill.
Not being at school.
Getting in trouble.
When somebody in my family dies.
When my friends run away from me.

Sarah Elizabeth Matthews (9)
Balbardie Primary School

MY LITTLE BROTHER

My little brother is a pest
He bugs me all day long
He bites my back
And kisses me
And that is why he is a pest.
And he also is quite clever
He can talk quite well
And turn the TV on and off
And I love him.

Fiona Cunningham (7)
Balbardie Primary School

HAPPINESS

Happiness is . . .
Going on holiday in the caravan,
Flinging snowballs that are very cold,
Swimming in the cool, sparkling water,
Relaxing in the hot, warm sun,
Skating on the slippy white ice,
Having fun with my friend,
Doing this till the very end.

Sadness is . . .
When my grandad died,
When I don't like something,
When I cry,
It's raining and starting to hail,
Doing things and getting them wrong,
Especially when I'm ill,
But most of the time I'm happy.

Stephanie Louise Murphy (9)
Balbardie Primary School

MY FAVOURITE FOOD

Bread and soup smells great,
It tastes delicious on a plate,
It looks brilliant,
When it is cooking it makes me hungry,
If I touch it, it feels funny,
When I eat it, it goes in my tummy.
I feel warm
I do like soup.

Stacey Roy (8)
Balbardie Primary School

HAPPINESS

Happiness is . . .
Swimming in the cool, bubbly water,
Scoring lots of goals and everyone cheering,
Playing the Playstation and winning the game,
Watching funny programmes,
Drawing myself in my room,
Meeting more friends
When I sing a hymn in the hall.

Sadness is . . .
Falling out with my friends,
When my team loses at football,
When my mummy is away on holiday,
When my grandad died,
Having a row,
Making mistakes in my work.

Drew Anderson (9)
Balbardie Primary School

ANT

Ants are fast, speedy, quick to move.
Ants you can lift heavy things.
So that means they are tough and strong.
Ants can bite and nibble.
Ants are tiny little creatures.
Ants can be all different colours.
Like brown and black or brown and red.
Ants, I think they look nice.

Kimberley Jarvis (8)
Balbardie Primary School

THROUGH THAT DOOR

Through that door are little, bright stars.
Funny looking aliens.
Spaceships travelling from planet to planet.
Moon buggies bumping over the rocky surface.
Comets leaving a trail of dust.
Astronauts floating in space.

Skye Stacey (8)
Balbardie Primary School

THROUGH THAT DOOR

Through that door in a city with lots of lights.
In that city there are places with incredible heights.
In that city there are shops and roads with lots of cars.
There are lots of noises.
In that city there are houses.

Leanne Maitland (8)
Balbardie Primary School

THROUGH THAT DOOR

Through that door
Is a planet with huge craters.
An enormous grey spaceship with big clear windows.
A big, green alien coming out of the door
Bright, shiny stars
A lovely, round, smiling moon.

Laurie Innes (8)
Balbardie Primary School

ANT

Ant, you are so bad.
Ant, I don't like you because you attack the leaves,
Ant, you're fast. Your speed is like a cheetah.
Ant, you scuttle so quickly.
Ant, you're so strong and tough to chew, munch and nibble.
Ant, you crunch leaves even though you are so small.
Ant, you're so little and tiny.
Ant, you have dull colours like red, black and brown.

Christopher Whyte (7)
Balbardie Primary School

ANT

Ant, you are fast, speedy and quick to move.
Ants munch.
Ants dribble.
Ants nibble.
Ants chew.
Ants crunch.

Nicola Parker (7)
Balbardie Primary School

ANT

Ant, you are fast, speedy and quick to move
Ant, you are strong and tough.
You munch, crunch, nibble and chew.
I can hardly see you because you are small.
You are brown,
You can be red
I like you, ant.

Robyn Young (7)
Balbardie Primary School

THROUGH THAT DOOR

Through that door,
Is a jungle with trees, green and growing tall.
Birds beautifully coloured, flying in the sky,
Not a house to be seen at all.
Animals making strange noises,
Flowers, colourful and poisonous next to a strange pool,
Snakes slithering through the jungle very scary,
Waterfalls enormous and cool.

Christopher Hill (8)
Balbardie Primary School

ANT

Ant, you're fast, speedy, quick to move.
Ant, you're strong and tough.
When you bite you nibble and crunch.
You're small, little and tiny.
Ant, you're black and you have eight legs.
You have a big hump at the back and a little hump at the front.

Sean Duncan (7)
Balbardie Primary School

SNAKES

Snakes are slithery
Snakes can climb.
Snakes are slimy.
Snakes are poisonous.
Snakes can bite.
Snakes like mice.

Aaron Stewart (7)
Balbardie Primary School

MY ANIMAL POEM

Sheepdog rounding up sheep
Heavy sheepdog getting tired
Eating its food
Excitement is coming
Playing with its pups
Deeply asleep
On the mat
Groaning and dreaming.

Steven McDonald (8)
Balbardie Primary School

FOOTBALL

Football is good
On the ball all the time.
On the ball all the time.
The game is hard
But we tried
All the time
Long ball up the wing
Lucky we never lost.

Calum Ferguson (7)
Balbardie Primary School

MY ANIMAL POEM

Dozy duck,
Unhappy,
Crying in the cornfield,
Kind farmer finds him.

Gavin Ross (8)
Balbardie Primary School

THROUGH THAT DOOR

Through that door
Is a city of gold,
Sparkling cars,
Twinkling windows,
Glittering pavements,
Valuable houses,
Glamorous shops,
I wish I lived here.

David Simmonds (8)
Balbardie Primary School

THROUGH THAT DOOR

Through that door is an ocean floor.
Fish swim about.
An octopus waving its tentacles.
A shark showing sharp teeth.
I see divers.
The plants wave about.
Floating jellyfish.

Gillian Fleming (8)
Balbardie Primary School

THROUGH THAT DOOR

Through that door is a fantasy world
With pop stars singing and leaping.
People opening funfairs
Children jumping and laughing
Dancers dancing all around with soft ballet shoes.

Stephanie Macfarlane (8)
Balbardie Primary School

THROUGH THAT DOOR

Through that door is outer space
Aliens, horrible, slimy and green.
Really terrifying.
Friendly spacemen exploring in rockets.
Yellow moon, glowing and shining
High up in the sky.
Hot sun, glowing and moving.

Melody Sloan (8)
Balbardie Primary School

THROUGH THAT DOOR

Through that door is space,
Aliens with green and purple skin,
Happy and giggling.
A planet with strange holes,
An enormous spaceship,
Lots of planets spinning.

Kimberley Mollon (8)
Balbardie Primary School

THROUGH THAT DOOR

Through that door is a ruined house,
With lots of mice.
No carpets at all.
Bees buzzing all around with red and yellow stripes.
Ruined walls with no wallpaper anywhere.

David Greig (8)
Balbardie Primary School

MY SISTER

My sister Jennifer is only three
And thinks she knows more than me.
She likes Action Man toys that are made for boys.
But most of all she likes all my toys.
She loves Tigger and Piglet and Winnie The Pooh
And every day says she wants to go to the zoo.
Her hair tickles my nose when she sleeps in my bed.
My sister Jennifer is my best friend.

Callai Lochran (7)
Balbardie Primary School

FAMILY

Families are very nice and kind all the time.
Mums and dads give us healthy food
In the morning I like to play with my brothers.
Later on we go outside
Yes, I love my family.
Seven people in my family.

David Ferguson (7)
Balbardie Primary School

THE LOVELY GIRL

I knew a girl called Clare she was a pest.
Every time I go for her she played with me.
She followed me, she stayed for tea.
She sat beside me.
It was annoying.

Clare Farrell (7)
Balbardie Primary School

RUBBISH

R educe, reuse, recycle.
U sually you can.
B ig boxes can be flattened.
B ottles can be banked.
I could throw away less.
S o could you.
H elp us solve the problem.

Graham Dymock (8)
Balbardie Primary School

RUBBISH

R otting, reeking, rubbish.
U gly unpleasant smells.
B ig bits and little bits.
B infuls and bagfuls.
I nquisitive invading flies.
S urround the stinking stacks.
H eaped everywhere in the tip.

Rachel Allan (8)
Balbardie Primary School

FOOTY

F ooty is fun.
O n the ball.
O n the ball.
T o player to player
Y es it's a goal!

Alasdair Binnie (8)
Balbardie Primary School

RUBBISH

R ubbish on the street
U sually dropped by a litterbug.
B ut he'll get caught one day
B ecause we're after him!
I t's not right to drop rubbish
S o pick it up - *now!*
H elp keep our street tidy!

Darren Whigham (8)
Balbardie Primary School

LITTER

L ots and lots of it!
I n every corner of the park.
T houghtless people have done this.
T oo silly to care.
E ach piece dropped
R uins another bit of this beautiful park.

Graeme Mackenzie (8)
Balbardie Primary School

MY KITTY CAT

K itty come on Kitty come on I will give you a treat.
I love you Kitty Cat very much.
T iny little Kitty Cat everyone loves you.
T iny little Kitty Cat, hang out with all your friends.
Y eah! You can jump very high. I love you little Kitty.

Lauren Barclay (7)
Balbardie Primary School

Robyn's Poem

High in the mountains
In Wester Ross
There lived a dog
Who was very cross.
He had a sore paw
And could not run fast
On the hills with the sheep
This sheepdog was last.
One day he woke up
The pain had all gone
And all of the sheep
Were penned up before long.

Robyn Caldwell (7)
Balbardie Primary School

Rubbish

R olled up and crumpled in the street
U p it flies in the wind
B ig bits and little bits.
B lack bits and white bits.
I t looks so bad.
S uch a shame!
H ow can people be so silly?

Scott Morrison (9)
Balbardie Primary School

ANIMALS

A nimals are cute creatures
N igeria in Africa has lots of wild animals
I like all types of animals
M y favourite animal is a kangaroo
A ligators have very sharp teeth
L ions are the king of the jungle.

Rachel Cooper (7)
Balbardie Primary School

ORANGE

Mouth-watering
Bumpy
Squelchy
Juicy
It makes my mouth watery.

Greig Kay (11)
Balbardie Primary School

GRAPES

Fat
Smooth
Squishy
Sweet
It makes my mouth fresh.

Christopher Kennedy (12)
Balbardie Primary School

LITTER

L ots of it all around us.
I n the parks in the gardens, in the street.
T oo many litterbugs.
T oo few litter detectives.
E veryone could help if they wanted.
R emember! It's easy to use a bin.

Laura Miller (8)
Balbardie Primary School

LITTER

L itter is a horrible thing.
I t is really smelly too.
T ips are full of it.
T rucks come to collect it.
E verybody tries not to drop it.
R ubbish is its other name.

Callum Stewart (8)
Balbardie Primary School

LITTER

L ots of paper
I n the playground.
T oo many people
T oo lazy to find the bins.
E veryone knows where they are.
R emember to use them please.

Mandy Strachan (8)
Balbardie Primary School

RUBBISH

R ubbish can be all sorts of things.
U sually scraps of food, paper and cans.
B ig piles outside houses.
B in men collect it.
I t is taken to the dump.
S quashed by machines.
H uge and noisy.

Laura Sim (8)
Balbardie Primary School

RUBBISH

R ubbish, rubbish everywhere
U nder your feet.
B e careful not to slip.
B e careful not to fall.
I can't understand why we do this at all.
S uch a shame to spoil our town.
H ow could we let it happen?

Chloe Whiteside (8)
Balbardie Primary School

LITTER

L itter can be smelly.
I t sometimes attracts rats.
T oo many people just don't bother
T o use the bins
E ven though they see them.
R esult - *mess!*

Emma Pringle (8)
Balbardie Primary School

LITTER

L ots of it thrown about
I n the playground, in the street.
T hink about the mess it makes.
T erribly untidy.
E verybody should use the bins.
R emember the bottle banks too.

Cheryl Mochrie (8)
Balbardie Primary School

THE BOY THAT HAD THE FLU

There was a boy called Lou
Who thought he had the flu
With a cough and a sneeze
And a great big wheeze
His nose was all red
So he went to bed.

Stephanie Wood (9)
Colinton Primary School

A DARK FOGGY NIGHT

It's a dark, foggy day and a boy called Colin is out to play.
It's so dark he looks at a grey tree blowing around like a bumble-bee.
Everything seems so quiet, everything usually makes a riot
But now it's so peaceful so *shshshshshsh.*

Cameron Gaff (10)
Colinton Primary School

MY HORSE

I like to imagine . . .
Riding in the countryside
On a hot summer's day,
When the wind whistled and the trees blew.

My horse gallops through the green grass,
His coat shines in the sun,
His hooves trot rhythmically down the lanes,
I love him oh so much . . .
Then when I put him away at night,
I thank him with a hug,
I leave him to rest in his stable,
And I dream again of riding him.

Rachael Mary Kirk (9)
Colinton Primary School

A MOOSE

The moose stands at the top of the mountain high
And looks down at the flowing river below
As he stands so proud up high
As he is the king so he cannot sigh
When he stands up there so proud
Shouting out I am the king
So as he stands up there so proud
Thinking I am the king, I am the king.

Michael Macfarlane (10)
Colinton Primary School

MY DAD'S WORK

My dad's work
is a nasty place,
you're locked up in an office
until daybreak,
and you try to escape
but you never get past the
guarded gates.

My dad's work
is packed with men,
not a woman in sight,
and they all have a pen,
why I diney ken
but why do they work there?
Must need the care.

James John Carr (10)
Colinton Primary School

MR SMURFY

My name is Mr Smurfy.
I come from Smurfland.
He's Papa Smurf.
He is the best and nicest.
I like Papa Smurf.
He is the champ.

Muzamel Amjed (9)
Colinton Primary School

THE GIVING SAINTS

Do not stand by my grave and cry,
I am not there. I did not die.
I am the autumn wind that blows in and out of trees.
I am the sunshine for all to see.
I am the water that drips down to the sea.
I am the swan, so graceful in sight.
Animals frolic everywhere and I say, I did care.
I am the lion so proud and untamed,
So do not stand by my grave,
I am not there,
I did not die,
I am everywhere.

Scott Dowd (10)
Colinton Primary School

LIFE AND DEATH

Life sometimes makes you cry,
It sometimes seems unfair,
However small or down you feel,
You never should despair.

Death conquers over all,
It makes everybody equal,
However poor or rich
You are, it conquers all.

Daniel Rhymes (10)
Colinton Primary School

THE FOREST

The dark gloomy forest, so peaceful, so quiet
The towering forest leaning over the silent, golden grass
The shady, scary forest with eyes burning behind the black, broken,
old trees
The peaceful wind flowing in and out of the shady, towering, dark,
gloomy forest.

Murray Poole (11)
Colinton Primary School

CELEBRATION 2000

The Millennium Bug
the Millennium Dome
all of the celebrations
in London and Rome.

Euro 2000
the Olympic Games
all of the people
who want to be in fame.

Brilliant fireworks
festivals and parties
and eating lots of
purple Smarties.

It's so cool
when drinking rum
everyone it's
the millennium!

Fraser Pirie (9)
Cramond Primary School

WAR

War is a thing
No one can understand,
When they murder your family
And your enlistment they demand.

When people don't choose peace
And choose to be bombed instead,
It really makes the cog wheels
Whirl and twirl in my head.

There are so many ifs and buts,
It's hard to comprehend,
But if we found a cure,
It would surely end.

But sadly there's no cure for war
And maybe there would be,
It gets to be a rotten bore,
If only world leaders could see.

The money we spend on planes and ships,
On shells and tanks and bombs,
We could be using to help developing countries,
People in need, the homeless, and single moms.

Mike Nowiszewski (11)
Cramond Primary School

CELEBRATION 2000

The year 2000 is coming soon
Sing a song, play a tune
Do the conga, stand in line
Kick out your legs, it will be just fine.

Here comes the millennium, it's very near
All the drunks will be full of beer
Open your mouth and let out a cheer
Come on everybody, the millennium's here.

Katie Buchanan (9)
Cramond Primary School

MILLENNIUM 2000!

The millennium is coming,
let's give out a cheer,
what's going to happen?
Well, open your ears.

Could Martians be coming?
Will new planets appear?
Will futuristic things happen?
Don't spread any fear.

The unknown might come
in a big rocket ship,
they might take a person,
the person might give them a tip!

We might be living on Mars?
Or Venus?
Maybe still Earth?
I don't know.
A mini Nasa in Perth?

The millennium is near,
so give out a cheer,
I don't know what will happen,
this is just an idea.

Naomi Gibson (10)
Cramond Primary School

CELEBRATE THE YEAR 2000

The Millennium Dome has been built
World records being made
And new discoveries
So come along and celebrate
The year 2000

There's a new Scottish parliament
Parades everywhere
And conga lines all over the world
So come along and celebrate
The year 2000

There's going to be darkness everywhere
Festivals too
And there might even be a world war three
So come along and celebrate
The year 2000.

Hari Sukarjo (9)
Cramond Primary School

MILLENNIUM 2000

There was a young girl called
Anne Tousand,
and she went to the celebration
two thousand,
she saw a firework,
and went berserk,
and that is the story of
Anne Tousand.

Catherine Atterton (9)
Cramond Primary School

MILLENNIUM

The year 2000
Oh, I can't wait
Lots of parties all around
Maybe some time capsules to be found
More discoveries all about
When the clock strikes 12, give out a shout
Lots of fireworks on New Year's Eve
Lots of presents being received
Some world records might be broken
Give me a New Year's party token
Darkness and powercuts on the New Year
Oh dear me, we're full of fear
That's it for now, bye with a tear.

Ailsa Jack (9)
Cramond Primary School

CELEBRATION 2000, OR WILL IT?

Celebration 2000 all the fear unknown
What is going to happen?
No one really knows.
Will Arthur's seat erupt?
Will there be no more?
What if disaster strikes?
World War Three?
You've got to evacuate me,
But I hope for parties and stuff,
For Scotland to win the Euro Cup,
That would be my year 2000.

Stuart Brown (9)
Cramond Primary School

CELEBRATION 2000

It's nearly midnight,
It's giving me a fright
The year 2000
Oh what a sight!

It's getting dark
But the future's getting light
Strike, ah! the lights have gone out,
I can't see
So please don't hurt me
It gave me a fright
I can't wait until it's light.

Craig Macpherson (10)
Cramond Primary School

CELEBRATION 2000

It's nearly the millennium
let's have a party
with fireworks
and fun.

It's nearly the millennium
a new beginning for everyone
let's sing and dance
and take a chance
and look forward to
the next one.

Lauren Chornogubsky (9)
Cramond Primary School

CELEBRATION 2000

Here comes the millennium,
so everybody let's have fun.
We can see the festivals and parties too,
we might even do the congo.
Happy people drinking beer,
so come on everybody,
three cheers for the millennium.

Gemma Thomson (9)
Cramond Primary School

CELEBRATION 2000

There was a young man called Townsend
Who joined celebration 2000
He was squashed flat
By a very fat cat
And that was the end of Townsend.

Robert Lyon (9)
Cramond Primary School

CELEBRATION 2000

There was a man from Sellennium
who went to see the millennium
a comet bashed his head
and now he's dead
that poor man from Sellennium.

Desmond Doran (9)
Cramond Primary School

CELEBRATION 2000

Celebration 2000
get ready for a new year.
Prepare for a big celebration,
a new beginning is here.
The school extension will soon be complete,
the parties are taking place.
Parades are all over the city,
And everyone's full of grace.
The Millennium Bug is coming,
the computers will be confused.
In the night there might be power cuts,
so electricity can't be used.
Fireworks shoot to the skies,
they're beautiful through everyone's eyes.
But I think no one's realising,
That the millennium's very exciting.

Calum Boyce (9)
Cramond Primary School

CELEBRATION 2000

There'll be parties, parades
and festivals, yeah.
Holidays will be fully booked,
the Millennium Dome will
have a new look.
Fireworks, conga and a pint of beer,
that's my New Year!

Michael Logue (9)
Cramond Primary School

CELEBRATION 2000

What will happen on the year 2000?
Nobody knows,
Stunts and festivals, parties as well,
World records or snow,
Fireworks, parades, holidays too,
Extinction or even millennium flu.

James Macnaughton (10)
Cramond Primary School

CELEBRATION 2000

There was a man from home
who said, 'Oh look there's the Millennium Dome'
he banged his head
now he's dead
poor man who saw the Millennium Dome.

Aaron Foreman (9)
Cramond Primary School

CELEBRATION 2000

There was a Millennium Bug
who looked a lot like a slug
he ate alien chips
and flew in spaceships
and that was the Millennium Bug.

Alex Targowski (9)
Cramond Primary School

CELEBRATION 2000!

New school building,
Tragedy,
Crashed computers,
Not for me!

New discoveries,
Inventions too,
Live on Mars,
Just me and you.

The ozone is ruined,
By CFCs,
To put it together,
Be in more than 3s.

Katherine Goudie (9)
Cramond Primary School

CELEBRATION 2000

C is for the crashed computer in the year 2000
E veryone is having a party
L ights are out and it is dark
E veryone is happy and having a good time
B ig celebration
R obots are everywhere in Scotland
A ircraft 2000
T here are aliens in Scotland
I nvisible in town
O zone disasters
N ew discovery.

Omeair Saeed (10)
Cramond Primary School

MILLENNIUM BUG

The Millennium Bug
Is a horrible thing,
It's in your computers
And badness it will bring.

Oh how I hate
The Millennium Bug,
It ruins our electricity
And nibbles on your rug.

The Millennium Bug
Everyone hates,
It's in your Gameboy
And even on your plates.

Joanna Highton (9)
Cramond Primary School

CELEBRATION 2000

C rashed computers
E xciting
L ights are out
E verybody have a good time
B ugs in computers
R obots everywhere
A new beginning
T he day of tomorrow
I nvisible
O range food
N ew discoveries.

Liam Blaikie (9)
Cramond Primary School

CELEBRATION 2000

The New Year has come,
This is a very special one
Because it is the millennium.

What is going to happen?
I don't know.
Will it snow
Or will everybody have to go?

Will everybody start to fight?
In that night
Will there never be light?

The Olympics are going to come
And some football, oh what fun.

The New Year has come,
This is a very special one
Because it is the millennium.

Daniel Guild (9)
Cramond Primary School

THE MILLENNIUM BUG 2000

Bugs, bugs, they're coming out to destroy the network,
No, no, don't do that,
Oh look, there's a virus on the PC,
Help, help, what shall I do?
What shall I do?
Oh no, there's no heating and no electricity!
What shall we do? The bugs are back and they're here to stay.

Jamie Hamilton (9)
Cramond Primary School

MILLENNIUM 2000

The millennium is coming
It's almost here
Let's give out a shout
Let's give out a cheer

What's going to happen?
I don't really know
Instead of having summer
We could have months of snow!

Perhaps we'll find new planets
Or Martians on stars
Maybe we'll live on Uranus
Or the superdy duperdy Mars

Will any of this happen?
I don't know
The world might freeze with a lot of snow
If it did happen
A lot of people would say, 'Oh no!'
But maybe instead
It will be a big yellow glow.

Helen Robson (9)
Cramond Primary School

MILLENNIUM BUG

I hate the Millennium Bug, it is stupid
I hate the Millennium, it is dumb
I hate the Millennium, everything will go wrong
I hate the Mmillennium, my computer will go wrong
I hate the Millennium, everyone will go mad.

Geoff Melrose (9)
Cramond Primary School

CELEBRATING THE YEAR 2000

Celebrating 2000 years, shouting and yelling,
drinking and hangovers.
Celebrating 2000 years, the town is busy,
our house is full.
Celebrating 2000 years, I do not know how long
this will go on for! Two weeks?
People are singing songs.
Celebrating 2000 years, everyone stays
up all night, they are sleepy in the morning,
but still celebrate the millennium.
Celebrating 2000 years, there is a bug
going round my house switching off lights
and computers.
Celebrating 2000 years, what is going on?
It is confusing me.
Celebrating 2000 years.

Marianne McIvor (9)
Cramond Primary School

WOULD YOU?

Would you? Could you? Celebrate
I wouldn't, I couldn't celebrate, not in a box,
Not in a tree, I won't celebrate, don't you see?
Just celebrate here or there, I won't celebrate anywhere,
Not in a car, not in a train, I'll never celebrate,
Not in the dark, not in the park, I don't want to celebrate.

Matthew Ritchie (9)
Cramond Primary School

STREET PARTIES

Edinburgh is having a party,
with lights and gold and silver fireworks.
There's rides that bump and thump,
and gleam in the jet-black sky,
people eating apple pie,
people crowding all the streets,
eating lots of lovely treats.

There's people drinking in the pub,
plus people dancing in a club.
There's flashing lights and loud music,
entertainers doing a trick.
This celebration will last for days,
people serving food on trays,
so come and join us in the streets
and eat all of the lovely treats!

Laura Russell (9)
Cramond Primary School

STREET PARTY

Street parties are lots of fun
They have music and thousands of people
Loads of people think about stupid things like spending too much
Money
And some stupid people drink and get drunk.

There are fun bits for children
Bouncy castles for them and a crazy cottage for them as well
Children spend a lot at the fair and at the shops
The same as me.

James Samain (9)
Cramond Primary School

MILLENNIUM BUG

I really hate the Millennium Bug,
It crawls into my computer and makes itself snug!

My computer doesn't work anymore,
I feel like throwing it across the floor.

My mum just got me a new PC,
Then that Bug started to annoy *me!*

It crawled around, then into my ear,
It was so swollen up, I really couldn't hear.

So, after three days . . .
I sat on it!

Katy Nowiszewski (9)
Cramond Primary School

BUG

My computer is very nice,
Bang! Bang! Buzz! Buzz!
I especially like the games,
Bang! Bang! Buzz! Buzz!

What's happening to it?
Bang! Bang! Buzz! Buzz!
Oh no! Our computer has got a virus.
Bang! Bang! Buzz! Buzz!
The Millennium Bug has bitten!

Stuart Hope (9)
Cramond Primary School

MILLENNIUM

It's time to celebrate and lots of people cannot wait
for the year 2000 there will be entertainers
and no complainers because the millennium is here.

Lots of buildings will be built, such as the Dome
and the new parliament, our school's building work
will go on and standing there on show our new school's
extension will be there and excitement will be everywhere.

The only problem that will remain is the Millennium Bug
oh what a pain! There will be fireworks going off in the street
and men in the pub will meet. You're at home - but all of a sudden,
your computer explodes, oh no, it's the Millennium Bug!

Angeline Benge (9)
Cramond Primary School

MILLENNIUM PARTY

The millennium party will be fun
Lots of sweets, yum, yum, yum.
Princes Street and round the castle
There will be such a lot of hassle.

But it will not all be fun and hugs,
There will be the Millennium Bugs.
It might even ruin my computer
And it will happen in the future.

Gordon Shishodia (9)
Cramond Primary School

1ST JANUARY 2000

On the 1st of January 2000
everyone will go mad and drink too much beer
and have hangovers, people want to get married and have babies.
There will be street parties, and pubs will be full.
Everyone will be lucky to be alive at the millennium.
Computers will have bugs chewing at their wires,
computers might explode.
There will be fireworks with big bangs
and bright colours with sparks flying in the air.
It will be special, there will be lots of parties and discos.
I will be ten next year,
some people are really excited, but I'm not bothered.

Alice Walton (9)
Cramond Primary School

PARTIES

There is going to be a huge party
Can you guess what it is?
People will celebrate with champagne and wine
Can you guess what it is?

There will be lots of people in Edinburgh
Can you guess what it is?
People will be very happy when it comes
Can you guess what it is?
The millennium.

Sandy Richardson (9)
Cramond Primary School

CELEBRATION 2000

Go to Edinburgh where there's shouts and cheers,
Or go to London with English peers.
The fireworks go off,
The Dome goes on.

Fireworks lighting the sky,
Five seconds to go 4, 3, 2, 1.
The old year has gone, bye,
Somebody shouts I want a bun.

It will be as exciting as space,
See the worry on my face.
A new start
And a new generation of football stars.

Niall Cameron (10)
Cramond Primary School

THE PUB BUG

I saw a bug in the pub
and I put it in a jug.
I put the jug on the rug
but the bug goes out of
the jug and the mug
but the bug jumped in
to the jug and
the mug but the
jug and the mug
smashed in half.

Chris Casciani (9)
Cramond Primary School

CELEBRATION 2000

I was in the street partying, waiting for 12 o'clock,
I was drinking, shouting, waiting for twelve o'clock,
I was watching fireworks and waiting for twelve o'clock,
I was counting down but waiting for twelve o'clock.
Then the waiting was over, great cheers went up, millennium,
millennium.
So I went down to the centre of Edinburgh, suddenly the lights went
out and we all began to shout.
I knew it was the Bug, the Millennium Bug, could he be hiding under
a rug?
Suddenly the lights went back on, the Bug was gone.
I was wondering what the future would hold, could it be told?
Maybe new animals, new species, *bang* another firework dazzled the
sky with orange, pink, blue, red and yellow sparks bigger than your eye.
All the waiting and debating that the world has done, will this be a
great millennium?

Grant Stewart (10)
Cramond Primary School

MILLENNIUM BUG

The Millennium Bug crawls all about,
He lives in computers,
Where other bugs stroll around,
The Millennium Bug hides away until the day,
Millennium! To play around with his friends
To sing a song, millennium!

Alexandra Grahame (9)
Cramond Primary School

CELEBRATION 2000

It's millennium 2000, in Edinburgh
all the streets are mobbed with people full of excitement and happiness.
People dancing to music, the air is full of smoke and smells from the
barbecue and food stalls.

The noise is horrendously loud with, music,
shouting, laughing and singing.

The fireworks are about to begin.
People come and sit down and watch them. *Bang!*
The fireworks have begun successfully, everyone jumped
and started to clap their hands. the huge, huge colourful lights of
the fireworks were amazingly bright.

It is nearly time for us to go but, never mind.
I am really tired and exhausted, but other people
will stay and party all night.

Lauren Graham (11)
Cramond Primary School

CELEBRATION 2000

We will all remember what happened in the last 1000 years,
War, disasters, but that's all gone. It is the year 2000.
In every house a party, in most streets crowds are gathering.
Fireworks light up the night sky. It's the countdown, New York,
Edinburgh, London all waiting.
The bells ring and guns fire. Music, we all get dancing, we all kiss.
What about the future? Will we live on the moon? Will we have
hover-cars and school trips to Pluto?
All we know is the millennium is the biggest party yet!

John Clark (11)
Cramond Primary School

CELEBRATION 2000

It's 11:00 pm, oooohhhh still another hour,
I know, I'll take a shower.
When I was in the shower it was as cold as ice
but, still very nice.
When I got out it was 11:30
so I went to check on my dog Berty.
Then I asked my sister Emma, if she wanted to play a game,
but she said, 'Can we play the game Insane?'
'Ok,' I said.
When we were playing Insane our mum said,
'Come on it's 11:59 pm look the new century's coming.'
Then before I knew it, it was 12:00, all the fireworks went off,
then all my mum's friends piled in the door.
She said, 'There were only going to be four!'
It was as noisy as a zoo!

Lauren Claire Dickson (10)
Cramond Primary School

CELEBRATION 2000

The second has changed, the minute has changed,
so has the hour, the day and the year. It's now the millennium!
The millennium, the millennium!
A time of grief, excitment and happiness.
A time of sorrow and to put back all the bad times.

There will be parties, there will be drinks, loads of
cheering and greeting.
There will be fights, there will be fireworks, so now it's the
millennium! The millennium, the millennium!

Lewis Wentworth (11)
Cramond Primary School

CELEBRATION 2000

Hovercrafts living in space,
this is in the future, plain as my face.
Robots are our slaves, living on the moon,
this is in the future, coming very soon.
Now is the millennium, this is now,
in the future you'll be saying wow!
Fantastic times, awful times, things you won't forget,
even if you lost the running at the Cramond fete.
But now we'll party and dance till dawn,
remembering people who are here and gone.
Watching amazing fireworks, drinking beer,
saying goodbye to the old year.

Daisy Robson (11)
Cramond Primary School

CELEBRATION 2000

Bright lights, beautiful colours, amazing fireworks,
all the people are so happy.
Having fun and drinking juice, just having a party.

Dancing to a band unknown, dancing hand in hand.
All the little children are so excited jumping up and down.

All this year I've been waiting for this day,
now it's over, I can't wait another year
and maybe next time I'll have a beer.

Eilidh Smith (11)
Cramond Primary School

CELEBRATION 2000!

I walk down the street not knowing what the future will hold.
The gypsies, the fortune tellers they shall be told.

But tonight in Edinburgh how will it be.
Celebration 2000 just wait and see.

The crowd, like raging elephants, pour into the streets,
Celebration 2000 here it meets.

Riot police cover all sides,
Celebration 2000 has no guides.

The clock is ticking, ten seconds to go,
Celebration 2000 friend or foe.

Year 2000 'Happy New Year' to you all,
Celebration 2000 has started a brawl.

The cramped up crowds all drunk and sore
Celebration 2000 brings an uproar.

The noise stronger than bulls
Celebration 2000 really rules.

As the crowd goes home not one of them is sober,
Celebration 2000 it still isn't over.

Three in the morning the cleaners all come,
Celebration 2000 is over and done.

Or is it?

Alexander McIvor (11)
Cramond Primary School

MILLENNIUM BUG!

It goes through our computers
making lots of trouble,
dislocating wires.
I've never seen this little bug
but I know it's there.
This bug is very sly,
it's very hard to catch.
Lots of people working,
trying to figure it out.
Who will be the one that
is the clever genius?
Will it be a man?
Will it be a woman?
Will it be in Britain?
Will it be in Spain?
Where will it be?
Who will it be?

Rebecca Mackenzie (8)
Cramond Primary School

CELEBRATION 2000

Many people will pitch a tent, on the street for this huge event!
The smells in the streets like hot-dogs and chips,
if you're really drunk, you'll give hefty tips!
The band still plays and the fireworks are bright,
all the colour and excitement is in your sight.
The night winds on, still dancing and singing,
now it's time to start a new beginning!

Ruraidh Robertson (10)
Cramond Primary School

CELEBRATION 2000

Dong! It's midnight, booms Big Ben,
Bang! It's midnight, booms the 1 o'clock gun.
We are in the twenty-first century
and the party's just begun.

The Millennium Bug will sweep the world
as lights go off, then on.
People will be drunk with joy
as today will have come and gone.

Bang! It's midnight, booms Big Ben,
Bang! It's midnight, booms the 1 o'clock gun.
We are in the twenty-first century
and the party's just begun.

The fireworks will be as bright as the sun
while I hug, and kiss my mum.
The Earth has been with us this long
and has two billion more years to come.

Bang! It's midnight, booms Big Ben,
Bang! It's midnight, booms the 1 o'clock gun.
We are in the twenty-first century
and the party's just begun.

Richard Lomax (10)
Cramond Primary School

FOOTBALL

Football is great fun,
the ball is like a bun.

Ronaldo is the best,
he's better than all the rest!

Zidane is French,
he's never on the bench!

Denilson is Brazilian,
he's worth 21 million!

Michael Craig (11)
Cramond Primary School

CELEBRATION 2000
Bang the clock strikes 12,
happiness in the streets,
fireworks loom overhead,
people partying and eating sweets,
but all the time without getting stopped
the Millennium Bug roams about.

Smells are wafting around,
fireflies zip about,
a bang and a flash start a new round,
boxers have millennium fights,
but all the time without getting stopped
the Millennium Bug roams about.

At home people are celebrating,
people are playing games,
someone's having a war or two
on their favourite computer game,
but the Millennium Bug's in the computer,
oh my gosh it's been shot by a tank.

A firework shoots into the air and explodes
into the year 2000.

Peter Goudie (11)
Cramond Primary School

2000

2000, 2000
From everything to the dome,
time capsules, new buildings
and the millennium gnome.

Shakespeare, Monet
There's a lot of things that happened.
Michaelangelo, Jesus
and Columbus, the captain.

Einstein, Millennium Bug
and the Vikings,
Washington, Churchill
and all the queens and kings.

Emma Connolly (9)
Cramond Primary School

THE MILLENNIUM GNOME

There is a gnome in my garden,
He is called the Millennium Gnome,
He lives beside the garden pond
And he has a special wand.
His wand is his fishing rod
Because every time he waves it he just nods.
And sometimes he gets lost you know,
So I have to call Gnome! Gnome! Gnome!

Rebecca Palmer (8)
Cramond Primary School

DINO 2000

There's a dino in my bed,
What can I do?
Can I take him to the circus
or can I take him to the zoo?
But he seems to like me and
my house too.
So I think I'll keep him here
with me and you,
But where can I keep him?
What can I do?
What can he eat?
Where can he go to the loo?
I'll keep him a secret so keep
quiet! Unless you decided
you wanted to buy it.

Melissa Chalmers (8)
Cramond Primary School

THE MILLENNIUM

The millennium is here, fireworks which are
bright and colourful so they light up the sky,
busy crowds swamp the streets.
Famous stars on the stage sing to their fans.

The bug is in the net waiting to pounce like
a vicious cat stalking a mouse.

The Millennium Dome has been built, it is
very famous now.

Graham Henderson (11)
Cramond Primary School

MILLENNIUM APPLE

Once I saw a big apple, it was as
big as an ordinary apple.
I wanted to buy it but I never had
enough money,
So I ran home as fast as I could.
But when I got back to the shops I
could not see it so I ran home sadly.
Then I looked in the fridge, there it was,
The Millennium Apple.
I asked my mum and said
'Mum where did this come from?'
She said, 'I bought it for you for
the millennium.'
'Thanks' I said, and I never whinged
again thanks to my mum and my apple.
So the next morning it was gone.
Not just that it's huge, oh right,
But I have to find it to show at school.
I need to find it today.

Janine McIntosh (9)
Cramond Primary School

MILLENNIUM BUG

Millennium is 2000, 2000 is a Bug, 2000 is the Bug's name,
the Bug is called 2000.
The Bug is a virus, the virus is a Bug.
Don't let the Bug near the PC, the PC is a mental box.
Here's a little secret, the Bug is a Martian from outer space.

Mary-Elizabeth Conn (8)
Cramond Primary School

TRAVELLING

Travelling is fun,
going to a country with lots of sun.

Travelling by aeroplane, boat or car
it can't have been that far.

Travelling, read a book, magazine or anything,
just do something to cover time.

Travelling, we're going now,
listen to the captain telling you how.

Engines start, fasten your belts,
here we go now.

Landing now, how time flies,
coming down from the skies.

Miami is the place to be
but I am overseas.

My holiday has begun,
it's time for some fun.

Katie Hamilton (11)
Cramond Primary School

MILLENNIUM BUG

My Millennium Bug eats the cable and the plug,
The Millennium Bug always drinking out of a mug,
And all he lives on is an electric plug.
I imagine it to be green and never ever to be seen,
I am not too keen to see someone green,
I have always imagined it to have a team.

Louise Macleod (9)
Cramond Primary School

THERE'S ONLY ONE MILLENNIUM GNOME

I have a gnome in my garden,
He's the biggest one there,
He has a little bow tie,
He's called the Millennium Gnome.
He has year 2000 on his hat,
He sits by my tree and I have a sign
up saying there's only one millennium
gnome, that's my one.
He looks at the fish swimming,
He tickles his chin and goes for a swim.
He's my millennium gnome.
He's a gnome and he's going to see the
Millennium Dome.
He's the millennium gnome and there's
only one of him.
Millennium, millennium, what will come next?
My grampa's old knickers or my dad's old vest.
What's so special about it?
What's going to happen?
What ever happens nothing's going to happen
to my millennium gnome.

Emma Dickson (9)
Cramond Primary School

CELEBRATION 2000

When I did a cough the computer turned off.
When I sang a song the computer turned on.
I told my pet slug and he said 'It's the Millennium Bug.'
I gave him a hug and ran.

Daniel Macnaughton (8)
Cramond Primary School

MILLENNIUM

Millennium is exciting and millennium is fun,
Millennium makes people happy,
Millennium makes people excited.
At millennium there will be a celebration for everyone.
Partying is groovy and partying is cool,
Partying makes people dance and partying makes people excited.
Most people like to party and I hope you do too.

Hayley Mills (8)
Cramond Primary School

MILLENNIUM

Millennium, millennium,
you are too cool, so why don't
you go swimming in a pool?
So now I know that you are not
cool because you won't go swimming
in a pool.

Catherine Anderson (8)
Cramond Primary School

THE MILLENNIUM

Mum, Mum look at the lights,
look how they zoom
through the sky.
Mum, Dad look how they twizzle
bright.

James Anderson (8)
Cramond Primary School

BULLYING POEM

There was once a girl called Sally
who was bullied and pushed in an alley.
She was feeling unwell,
thought she had to tell.
That was the girl called Sally.

There was a boy called Derek
who lived in a place called North Berwick.
He went away sad,
that bully went mad.
That was a boy called Derek.

There was a man called Sam
who was a very bad man.
He pushed and shoved
and then went thud.
That was the man called Sam.

Iram Shafi (11)
Cramond Primary School

SPACE VIEW OF THE MILLENNIUM DOME

Millennium Dome, Millennium Dome,
so small from up here,
sparkly and shiny
like the sun,
like a snowdrop in the sky.
I am so lucky I can see it every day
and night.

Angus Kennedy (8)
Cramond Primary School

SHADOW

My rabbit is black and white,
she bobs about in the night.

Shadow is her name,
she is very tame.

She likes to play tig
with her friends Fivel and Bigwig.

Shadow hates the vet
though he says she is his favourite pet.

She is a mother of five,
they were a handful but she survived.

I love Shadow and no one can take her away,
I love Shadow, I see her everyday.

Jenna Hall (11)
Cramond Primary School

WHY DO YOU BULLY?

Why do you bully?
It's wrong
Stop doing it
It keeps going on.

Nobody likes you
I'll tell on you
You're just making us feel sad
Why are you so bad?

I want to know why you bully me?
Leave me alone, you're hurting me, can't you see?

Gillian Fraser (11)
Cramond Primary School

THE MILLENNIUM BUG

Aaahh what's that?
It's a bug under my rug.
I better tug the rug.,
I pulled the rug, the bug came out.
I got a mug and put it on top of the bug,
The bug wiggled and twiggled and wiggled
until it stopped wiggling and twiggling
and wiggling.
Then I took it out and I thought it could
be my pet.
I said 'Pow' and the bug said 'Wow.'
Then the next morning, the bug went into
my computer,
Now it's called the Millennium Bug.
When I went on the computer I coughed and
the computer went off,
When I did a yawn the bug and the computer
went on.
I played on the computer, the bug kept on
getting in the way,
Then I tried taking it out and it came out.
Now it is still the Millennium Bug but it's
not in the computer.
It must be a magic bug.

Elizabeth Brown (8)
Cramond Primary School

DEATH

As I fly through the corridors,
Everything a blur,
Faces staring down at me,
My mind in a whirl.

I crash through some doors
And suddenly stop,
I hear them talking about my accident -
A hundred foot drop.

I remember that day,
Falling to the ground,
As I silently lay,
No one around.

But a passer-by,
Came and lay by me,
Pulled out their mobile
And called emergency.

So now I am here,
But the doctors give up,
I was here one minute,
But now my life's black.

Fiona Cameron (11)
Cramond Primary School

YEAR 2000

In the year 2000 there will be a blackout,
then there will be a shout from the people
watching TV and using computers, people
will say 'Hey! It's the Millennium Bug.'

Rhys-Owen Fisher (8)
Cramond Primary School

MILLENNIUM BUG

Millennium Bug you make me hungry
because domestic appliances will not feed my tummy.
Millennium Bug you might not make the car work
so I'll never get to Mars.
Millennium Bug what's that noise?
It's an aeroplane that can't fly.
Aahh it's a Millennium Bug, it's going to kill me.
I like computers but I hate Millennium Bugs because
my computer will not go to 2000.
Help!
When I was doing science Millennium Bug just cut
the cable and that was that.
Millennium Bug you make me glad, because the
school might not work I will not be sad.
Millennium Bug you might not make the bank make the money
ooow what shall we do.

Claire Smith (8)
Cramond Primary School

LOVE

Love is like a fire,
It seems it'll never end,
Going on and on until
the fire within burns out.
You'll never get back together,
As much as you try,
Your heart will be cold
until the next fire is alight.

Rachael Stewart (11)
Cramond Primary School

PLAYTIME!

One minute to go!
A second to go!
The bell has rung,
the waiting is done.
Quick get the ball you lot
or we won't get our favourite spot!
We got this pitch first,
you'll have to take the worst!
The teams are not right,
let's change them, is that all right?
When are we going to play?
Hopefully sometime today!
Mel got tackled by Jade,
she passed to Katie that was quite good.
Katie passes to Jen,
Jen waits and then
she shoots and scores
though we need more.
Kirsteen dribbles the ball
and passes to Fiona who is very tall.
Who passed to Mel,
who can tell,
will she score?
Oh no she scored!
We're not winning anymore,
I tripped and now my leg is sore.
There goes the bell,
they played very well,
in we go,
more work *oh no!*

Judith Telford (11)
Cramond Primary School

SUMMER

The end of term yippee,
Going to my friends to play,
The whole term is in the past,
No more maths at last.

Flowers, sun and buzzing bees,
Swimming in the salty seas,
Having water fights in the garden,
Oh no my ice-lolly's melting.

Sleeping in till 11.00am,
My brother playing in his den,
Playing with the rabbits in the run,
They were hopping about madly in the sun,
Then playing footie until day is done.

Summer is joyful and fun
And I can't wait for this one to come.

Emily Towns (11)
Cramond Primary School

NESSIE

I went tae Inverness tae see
A mysterious monster, a sea beastie,
It swims aroond the Loch O' Ness,
The tourists he is out tae impress.

No one knows if it's a Loon or a Jessie,
But all the locals call it Nessie,
It pops up here, it pops up there,
I think he does that for a dare.

Andrew Buchan (11)
Cramond Primary School

THE JUNGLE AND THE SEA

The jungle is a scary place,
But it also can be fun.
The jungle has brought us joy, will
you bring joy to the jungle?

The sea can be gentle when it's
lapping on the shore,
But it can be rough and tough
smashing on the rocks.
We can damage the sea, but remember
the sea can damage us.

You have heard things good and bad,
I'm going to help, are you?

Rosie Young (11)
Cramond Primary School

FROGS

Frogs are very wild
just like a three year old child.

Bouncing, hopping
don't go to school or do the shopping.

Swim all day
and don't have to pay.

I would like to be a frog,
well not an Australian frog.

They live in bogs!

Edward Grahame (11)
Cramond Primary School

THE TREE IN MY BACK GARDEN

The tree in my back garden is big, old and tall,
It flaps and dances in the wind, its branches clinging to its leaves so
                                                                    small.
Day by day it changes throughout the autumn time,
The leaves grow pale, red and brown and then fall to the ground.
But in the winter time when all its leaves have gone,
the branches finger my windowpane,
No leaves left to flutter down,
It's dark and brown and black, a shadow of the night.
But soon the spring will come again,
green buds will appear on the branches.
The leaves will grow back so green.
The tree in my back garden will start its year again another year older.
The tree in my back garden.

Elizabeth Craig (11)
Cramond Primary School

THE LOVE I GIVE

The love I give is strong as Earth,
as kind as heaven,
as loving as God.
The love I give is to you,
you I give, I give to you.
The love I give burns evil and blesses good
it does, it does,
it burns evil and blesses good.
The poem is mine and I give it to you,
I give, I give my true love to.

Kirsteen Paterson (11)
Cramond Primary School

MILLENNIUM BUG

There's something in your computer,
it's big, bright and green.

It lives on electricity but
it won't get an electric shock!

I hate this little critter, I hate
this little Bug.

He nibbles on the wires in your TV
so we can't watch it.

I hate him, I hate him.

If I was not human I would stick my
hand in the computer and put him on
a rocket up, up to Mars.

Stuart Mann (8)
Cramond Primary School

SCOTLAND

The haggis is a Scottish food,
I like it, it is very good,
It is made of oatmeal and sheep's belly,
And for my pudding I like some jelly.

The kilt is made from tartan of any kind,
Any shape or size that you can find.
The kilt is colourful and bright,
Men in skirts, what a funny sight.

Andrew Pringle (11)
Cramond Primary School

SUPPLY TEACHERS!

Small ones, tall ones,
fat and thin;

Dopey ones, blind ones,
kind ones done;

Old ones, young ones,
middle aged too;

Deaf ones, duff ones,
chuffed ones too;

Old fashioned with rations
for morning break;

And so we move on to
strict ones, nice ones,
and middle of the two;

Boring ones, happy ones,
sad ones true.

Christopher MacPherson (11)
Cramond Primary School

THE MILLENNIUM GNOME

I met a gnome in my garden,
He asked me what my name was.
I asked him right back.
'My name is 2000' said the gnome.
He jumped into a puddle and never
came back again.

Sarah Graham (8)
Cramond Primary School

2000 GNOME

There is a gnome in the garden home,
He stands still and his name is Bill.
He is in the mud and he looks so snug.
Now he is my gnome and I will never let him go home.
He is a little bit red and I am going to make him a bed.
He is also yellow and he sometimes makes me bellow.
He can't talk and he can walk,
And that's that end of my millennium gnome poem.

Abigail Farrer (8)
Cramond Primary School

2000

2000 is a number,
2000 is a date,
2000 can be anything,
as long as it can wait.
2000 after Christ,
2000 before me,
2000 years later it ended
up like this.

Rachel Gilchrist (8)
Cramond Primary School

MILLENNIUM 2000

Millennium Dome so big, never small, so white
on the top and a bit of yellow.
There will be so many interesting things inside,
it will be so busy.

Michael Forrest (8)
Cramond Primary School

THE MILLENNIUM BUG

The Millennium Bug is a creature,
you'll have to get close to feature.
To be so small and where you're going,
when it speeds up it comes down slowing.
To be better than a beetle and more important than a wasp.
It crawls on your back, it crawls in your hair,
I don't know where it's hiding, it's not the size of a bear.
The bug is here,
so give it a cheer,
I don't know what will happen, it's just an idea!

Colm Glackin (8)
Cramond Primary School

GNOME 2000!

There is a gnome in my garden,
He is small and round,
He carries a plaque that says 2000!
His name is Millennium,
I called him that.
He's laden with gold and not very old,
He's not very fat and lives on the mat!
We put him there because the mat says
'I'm a millennium gnome!'

Fiona Craig (8)
Cramond Primary School

THE RAINBOW

I saw a rainbow in the sky,
Its colours shining bright.
With red and orange and
Light, light yellow it was a very nice sight
And then came green and beside it came blue,
With indigo as dark as my shoe
And finally violet with its colour just right.
When suddenly, the colours all went,
For it was only the sun, beside a silly hose pipe!

Isla Wood (9)
East Calder Primary School

FOOTBALL

I am going to a football match,
I am going to see Rangers,
They scored 5 goals.
I am going to a football match next week,
I am going to see Scotland,
They scored 4 goals.
My dad is going to a football match,
He's going to see Celtic on Saturday,
They scored 5 goals.
I am going to a football match,
I am going to see Liverpool,
They scored 3 goals.
I went to a football match and Rangers lost,
I am never going to another match.

Leanne Pettigrew (10)
Eastertown Primary School

DISCO DIVA!

When you get glammed up to go disco dancing
And you feel that fab fever
You're delightful and dedicated
You're a diamond disco diva!

When you get your groove on up
Dance the night away
When you get that funky feeling
Just boogie, dance and play!

As you boogie all night long
Looking great in your glitzy, glamorous gown
Have fun grooving,
Just be a *dedicated disco diva!*

Karin Shanks (10)
Eastertown Primary School

CULMAILIE

I hear the water run so rapidly but quietly over the rough hard rocks.
I see the hill tops covered with snow so white, so cold.
I smell the fine hot vegetable soup, bubbling away on the hot fire in
a pot.
I feel happy, rich and very lucky.
I touch the sand but it slips softly and slowly through my fingers.
I taste the crunchy oatcakes with a layer of cheese on top, mmmm
delicious.
Culmailie so beautiful and the best home I have ever had.

Clare Ewen (10)
Eastertown Primary School

MY MUM IS ALWAYS SAYING . . .

My mum is always saying . . .
'Claire empty the dishwasher please
Make the dog's dinner
Set the table
Dust your dusty desk
Turn down your music
Stop shouting at your sister
Brush your teeth
Comb your hair
Do your homework,
                    Claire.'

Claire Brown (10)
Eastertown Primary School

I WANT TO PAINT A POEM

I want to paint my ugly bedroom door,
I want to paint the brilliant kitchen floor,
I want to paint a dark night,
I want to paint my sister in fright,
I want to paint a rainy day,
I want to paint a blue car roll away,
I want to paint the bathroom's boring walls,
I want to paint my little cousin's best dolls.

Kellie Smith (10)
Eastertown Primary School

GLASGOW POEM

I hear the gurgling
of factories
Smell the fish fresh
from the sea.
I touch cold metal of
the tenement door
I can still taste fresh
fish from Culmailie.
Nothing here is the same
as up at Culmalie.
Mum does not need to spin
wool anymore.
We don't need to go to the
stream for water.
I don't think I'll get
used to here.

Leeann Field (10)
Eastertown Primary School

MY MUM

My mum is small but very strong
She hoovers our house all day long.
She feeds me spaghetti and beans for dinner
If she was on 'Ready, Steady, Cook'
She wouldn't be the winner.
She's painted our walls bright, bright red
I would have preferred pink instead.
I know you think my mum's mad
Wait till I tell you about my dad!

Carrie Higgins (10)
Eastertown Primary School

I WANT TO PAINT!

I want to paint my boring bedroom walls
I want to paint a springtime daffodil
I want to paint all my best friends
So that the good times will never end!

I want to paint my large family
I want to paint an autumn tree
I want to paint my blue bike red
I want to paint everything in my head!

Deborah Elliott ((11)
Eastertown Primary School

I WANT TO PAINT A POEM

I want to paint my green bathroom walls.
I want to paint my boring ugly hall.
I want to paint a big fruit stall.
I want to paint my brother Paul.
I want to paint a new bright shawl.
I want to paint a bright lolly
I want to paint a gorgeous dolly.
I want to paint an autumn tree.
I want to paint everything.

Emma MacMillan (10)
Eastertown Primary School

MY BEST FRIEND

My best friend is a bit of a nutter
Because she sticks her head in butter.
Her name is Sandy
And she also likes Candy
She has a friend called Faye
And I've got to say she is a nice wee girl
But she's another friend called June
And it is her birthday soon
And she wishes she could go to the moon.

Stephanie Kidd (9)
Gorebridge Primary School

SPACE

S is for the stars that shine in the sky
P is for lots of planets in space
A is for the astronaut that lands on the moon
C is for computers in the spaceship
E is for exploring planets

Paula Scott (8)
Gorebridge Primary School

SPACE

S is for spacecrafts
P is for planets
A is for alert
C is for commander
E is for explore

Christopher Cornwall (8)
Gorebridge Primary School

MY FISH

I have two fish
That I wish
Would be a dish
For me to eat
Because they would taste so sweet.

I would have them with chips
Then lick my lips
I then was sick
Because they tasted sour
Because I ate their manure.

I got new fish
And I never wish
For me to eat them
And have that treat again
Of that disgusting dish.

Louise Brown (9)
Gorebridge Primary School

DOGS

Dogs are cute,
Dogs have different fur.
Dogs are fierce.
Dogs can run fast.
Dogs want outside every day
If dogs see cats they try and chase them.
Dogs are always hungry and want snacks off people.
Dogs watch you when you're eating
If dogs are sleeping, they sleep weird ways.

Colin Haddow (9)
Gorebridge Primary School

I'M TELLING ON YOU

I'm telling on you.
Why? Because you said I was untrue.
You're not untrue but I'm not telling on you.
Oh stop it, you two!
You're not untrue and he is not telling on you.
You are untrue but you can't have my shoe.
I'm telling on you
Why? Because you said I was untrue.

Stacey Schooler (9)
Gorebridge Primary School

STARS

S is for stars that shine so bright.
T is for take-offs.
A is for astronauts in space
R is for rockets all over the place
S is for spaceships in space.

Keith Black (8)
Gorebridge Primary School

SPECIAL POEM

S is for Saturn.
P is for Pluto.
A is for astronauts.
C is for captain
E is for emergency

Daryl Chisholm (9)
Gorebridge Primary School

THE HOLE

First thing after school I change
into my working gear and hard hat.
I drive a JCB and also a dumper
I dig a hole, it is ten metres deep
and it still has to go deeper.
I want to make a pool in it.
I hope to make a Jacuzzi
I will keep digging until I get to China
I like digging!

Allan Hall (10)
Gorebridge Primary School

MY BEST FRIENDS

My best friends are very, very kind,
They are very helpful and caring,
They help me if I'm stuck,
If I fell over or have nobody to play with.
When they see me all alone
They come and play with me.

Robyn Christine Warwick (9)
Gorebridge Primary School

SPACE

S is for stars that twinkle in the night
P is for places where nobody has been
A is for aliens who are unsuspecting
C is for comets which fly through the night
E is for explorers who explore in space.

Callie Loughrie (8)
Gorebridge Primary School

MY PETS

My pets
Are wet.
They're small and green
And they can hardly ever be seen
In supermarkets, stalls or shops,
But let me tell you, they're the tops!

You may think that they're fish,
But to fish they're a tasty dish.
They can grow one centimetre long
And their food has an awful pong.
As you can tell, they're very small,
But as they're small for their size
They're quite tall.

They're *sea monkeys*,
Not monkeys under the sea.
There are about 21
And they're doing fine.
If you saw them you would see,
Why they are perfect pets for me.

Emma Kent (9)
Gorebridge Primary School

LAZINESS

Laziness is blue
Laziness tastes like soup that's gone very cold
Laziness smells like burnt rubber
Laziness looks like not being bothered to get up
Laziness sounds like a man mumbling and grumbling
Laziness turns your legs to jelly.

Nicola Davidson (11)
Gorebridge Primary School

MY BEST FRIEND

My best friend, she is very funny,
She has a pet baby bunny.
One day the bunny got away
And with me came to stay.
It stayed for one whole month
And I gave it back the following night
And she never talked again to me
And I thought 'What have I done wrong?'

Kirsty Jack (9)
Gorebridge Primary School

SPACE

S is for the stars that twinkle so bright.
P is for the nine planets which light up at night
A is for the alert on the spaceship above
C is for the comets whizzing around
E is for the enemy whom I hope doesn't
                          come to our ground.

Sean Sweeney (8)
Gorebridge Primary School

HAPPINESS

Happiness is blue
It tastes like chicken curry
It smells like hazel
Happiness is like sunshine
It sounds like birds whistling
Happiness is like flying.

James Collins (11)
Gorebridge Primary School

MY TEACHER

My teacher is kind
but I don't mind.
But we don't get enough work
so give us work and wake up.
When she shouts, steam comes out her ears
and down her nose. She looks glum
and she looks like my mum.
She gives us work and shouts
I'm a teacher, you know!

Stewart Lithgow (9)
Gorebridge Primary School

LONELINESS

Loneliness is grey
It tastes like nothing on your plate
And smells like something that's not there
Loneliness looks like you're with someone but you're not
And sounds like a silent sound
Loneliness feels like thin air.

John Chisholm (10)
Gorebridge Primary School

HAPPINESS

Happiness is pink and yellow
It tastes like tropical fruit
And smells like summer's fresh air.
It looks like flowers appearing
It sounds like children in the park
And feels like being born again.

Nicola Graham (11)
Gorebridge Primary School

SPRING

Spring is a time of celebration
Spring is when the tulips grow
Easter is on its way
To have and to hold through
the good spring.
The sheep have lambs to
make more sheep and
bunny rabbits have bunnies
So spring is over
the fun has not stopped.
Summer is still to come!

Jillian McHale (9)
Gorebridge Primary School

GYM TIME

At gym my teacher says 'Jog on the spot!
Now run around the room!
Stop!
Start again!
Now put your left hand on the ground!
Get a partner!
Sit on the floor!
Stand up!
Jump up and down!
Now get changed!'

Lynsey Brown (8)
Gorebridge Primary School

HAPPINESS

Happiness is yellow.
It tastes like the sun
And smells like sticky toffee pudding.
Happiness looks like a day on the beach
And sounds like laughter and fun
Happiness is at the end of the day
                    in a nice hot relaxing bath.

Laura Herriot (11)
Gorebridge Primary School

HAPPINESS

Happiness is multicoloured,
It tastes like yummy strawberries
It smells like chocolate doughnuts,
It looks like a holiday theme park,
And sounds like an exciting computer game.
Happiness is like when the world
                    explodes into fun.

Dean Thomson (10)
Gorebridge Primary School

LAZINESS

Laziness is black.
It tastes like old soup
And smells like an unmade bed.
Laziness looks like somebody sleeping
And sounds like somebody snoring.
Laziness feels like the end of the world.

Kristofer Arthur (10)
Gorebridge Primary School

SPACE POEMS

S is for stars that twinkle so brightly
P is for a planet in space
A is for astronauts caught up in a race
C is for comets whizzing by, and last but not least.
E is for exploring into space.

Travelling deeper we go
How far are we from home, I don't know
I hope we are there
Not one more moment to spare
I am going up into Space.

Emma Drysdale (8)
Gorebridge Primary School

SPACE

S is for stars which shine so brightly
P is for planets which orbit round the universe
A is for astronauts who fly into space
C is for controls which tell you where to go
E is for exploring in space.

Travelling deeper we go
Into space my crew don't know
Engines blaring full of power
We're going into Space.

Michael Leitch (9)
Gorebridge Primary School

THE SILVER BIRCH

Silver birch, a tall tree,
As long as can be,
Its leaves so high in the sky,
Some I can't even see,
Its leaves are like gold
And I love to listen to the
Rustling noise it makes in the wind.
Its bark so pale,
When I look the thick sticks
That hold it so tight are so long.
The roots under the ground are so lumpy
But safe and sound.
I love to watch it,
The *Silver Birch*.

Sarah Paul (8)
Gorebridge Primary School

MY TEACHER

My teacher is nice
The teacher gives you work
That is why I'm not happy
'Cause I get so much work.
If you go to school
The teacher will give you work.
I like school because I love my teacher.
I like my friends, but most of all I
                           like the teacher.

Emma Todd (9)
Gorebridge Primary School

ME AND MY BROTHER IN THE MALL

Me and my brother
went to a mall,
to get a ball.
Once we got a ball
out of the mall,
I went flying,
so did the ball.
My brother said 'Wow!'
and chased the ball
after he got the ball
I tripped up on a stall
and met my friend Paul
he was Paul, Paul, Paul
so I flung the stall
on his small head
and said 'Wow!'
My brother had the ball
and ooh!
The mall was it all!

Ryan McNair (9)
Gorebridge Primary School

MY BEST FRIENDS

My best friends help me if I fall,
My best friends help me if I hurt myself
My best friends play with me when I am sad
Or have no one to play with.
I am very happy if they play with me.
I'd like to play with them if they would
                        like to play with me.

Sarah Frew (9)
Gorebridge Primary School

MY AUNTIE CORINNE

My Auntie Corinne,
She is fun and plays games with everyone,
I love my Auntie Corinne,
I've only stayed with her once,
She has brown hair,
I love her hair, it's so pretty,
She plays with me,
She loves my sisters the same as me,
People like her,
She says things like 'Would you like a drink?'
She buys me things for my birthday,
Her husband is called Peter,
I love him too,
So that's my Auntie Corinne,
She said I am pretty,
She tells me stories,
She said I could have anything to eat,
Oh, she loves me!
But the best thing is I love her.

Robyn Paul (8)
Gorebridge Primary School

COOL

It makes me cool when I see you drool
And when I'm in a swimming pool,
It is cool when you look like a fool
And you have a tool that is also a fool.
It makes me cool when you're as small as a stool,
And when your skin is as soft as wool,
It makes me cool when you bend the rule.

William Arthur (9)
Gorebridge Primary School

THE SILVER BIRCH

It sways in the wind.
It rustles around like maracas.
The roots dig deep like shovels.
The leaves like gold
Its branches like legs
In the winter the leaves fall
He's stripped of his clothes.

Nathan Ross Hammond (8)
Gorebridge Primary School

THE SILVER BIRCH

Golden branches
        brown bark
        bending branches that look
        like a long neck
        long stick-out roots
        that look like worms
        leaves brown and yellow.

Connie Blackhurst (8)
Gorebridge Primary School

CRICKET CREAK

Cricket, creak your rhythm song
Keep the birds, singing all day long
Creak, just tell me creak
Your lovely sound,
Just make me happy, creak
And we'll be sound asleep.

Michael Arthur (8)
Gorebridge Primary School

TINY MOUSE

A mouse's tail
Long and wiggly, squeak, squeak!
Small and round, squeak, squeak!
Quiet and round
Quiet and round

A mouse's body
Grey and pink, squeak, squeak!
Big big ears, squeak, squeak!
Quiet and round
Quiet and round.

Small
Really small feet, squeak, squeak!
Tiny toes, squeak, squeak!
Quiet and round
Quiet and round

The mouse . . . squeak, squeak!
In the house
Squeak, squeak, squeak!

***Emma Forrester* (8)**
Gorebridge Primary School

THE SILVER BIRCH

A tree is sometimes . . .
Long
Short
Bent
Some trees have thin branches
That look like hair.

***Kerry Turnbull* (8)**
Gorebridge Primary School

PE

My class and me
Went to PE
We threw a ball
Around the hall
We played hockey
Then pretended we were a jockey
We packed our shorts and T-shirts away,
Then worked for the rest of the day.

Cassie Fuller (8)
Gorebridge Primary School

DOGS

Some dogs go woof, woof!
And puppies go woof, woof!
And most of the time people buy daddy dogs.
So we have mostly daddy dogs
So woof, woof!
We have a woof woof
dirty woof woof
field woof woof.

Nicky Johnston (9)
Gorebridge Primary School

SWEETS

Candy sweets, chocolate crispies
lots of good things
nice to eat.
Candy bars, lollipops, Wispa bars!
Smarties, yellow, green and blue.
Lollies all shapes and sizes.
Trickel treat, chocolate bars,
they're all nice and
            good to eat.

Emma Hart (8)
Gorebridge Primary School

THE SILVER BIRCH

In the wind blows a shiny tree
Just like an old man flying like a plane
In the air leaves blowing like hair trunks
Fatter than a chair,
Roots stronger than the roots of hair.

Callum Rowley (8)
Gorebridge Primary School

Confusion - Future Past, Past Future?

I'm a little bit small, I'll be a little bit big,
I'm at school today, I'll be at work tomorrow,
I'm happy today, I'll be sad tomorrow,
I'm 10 today, I'll be 20 tomorrow.
It's the past today, it's the future tomorrow,
But where will I be, here or there?

I'm going to be big
And I'm going to work,
I'm going to be sad,
And I'm going to be 20,
This is my future or
Is this is my past.
I don't know, it's going too fast.

I'm going to be small
And I'm going to school,
I'm going to be happy
And I'm going to be 10,
This is my future or
Is this my past.
I don't know, it's going too fast.

Am I in the future or
Am I in the past?
I remember all the hard things,
But I can't remember that.
Is this my future or
Is this my past.
I don't remember, it's going too fast!

Liam Wilkinson (10)
Grange Primary School

CLASSROOM 2020

No teacher, just a boring robot,
Robot always shouts,
Which is different from Miss Campbell,
Because she's as quiet as a mouse.

No jotters, just laptop computers,
Which always bleep,
No blackboard, just a big TV ,
No library, just a computer.

She never tells us anything,
So we never know what to do,
Which is different from Miss Campbell,
Because she tells you what to do.

Ross Bell (9)
Grange Primary School

CLASSROOM 2020

No teachers to shout and bawl,
Just an old stiff and rusty robot,
Not so much writing and sums,
Working on PCs is so much fun.

We have blue uniform,
They may not,
They may have a different colour,
It may be even duller.

We have steel chairs with plastic,
They might have modern furniture,
They may have stools,
In all the different schools.

Kelly Stokes (10)
Grange Primary School

Sport

Football, football is my favourite sport,
Let me remind you never to play at an airport,
If you do we'll say bye-bye,
Your ball will maybe fly.

Hockey, hockey is a good game,
If you play you may have fame,
A good team like the Mighty Ducks,
Let me remind you, you play with pucks.

Basketball, basketball is a lot of fun,
You can play in the snow or sleet but best in the sun,
Let me remind you, be quite tall,
And also, you play with a bouncing ball.

Golf, golf is quite hard,
Your club should be metal, not card,
If you play, I hope you're good,
Remember, don't play in the nude.

Volleyball, volleyball is a super game,
Each side of the net is exactly the same,
I didn't play it as soon as it came,
Now I think it's a brilliant game.

Altogether, I think they're good,
I don't think any of them are really rude,
In years to come I hope they get better,
I also hope the sun makes it hotter,

Sports, sports you should play.
You'll become fitter, that's what the experts say.

Robert McClure (10)
Grange Primary School

THE SPACE RACE

In space there was a famous race,
All the people gathered up,
To see the famous racer, Zulan Zup.

He was a great galaxy racer,
He had lots of friends,
But the problem is, the fun never ends.

They all go into their places for the great galaxy races.

Zulan starts the race from last place,
First they fly around Jupiter, then around the sun.

Zulan moves into first place, and *crash!*
Don't worry it was just another racer,
Zulan wins the famous galaxy race.

Barrie Todd (11)
Grange Primary School

CLASSROOM 2020

First day at school,
No jotters but computers instead,
Hologramic teachers,
Where did Miss Campbell go?

Computers, computers typing away,
I'm going to school nearly every day,
I hate it when we have to go away,
Computers, computers keep typing today.

Working hard,
Laughing and shouting,
Making and mounting,
Loading and slowing.

No using pens,
But using computers,
Work, work, work,
I can't keep it up.

Fiona Jane Murray (10)
Grange Primary School

TELEPHONES

Telephones, telephones, talk, talk, talk,
Telephones you can use,
When you're out for a walk.

Small, handy, colourful, pocket sized and wee,
But every telephone
Looks boring to me.

I hope in the future telephones will be better,
I hope you will be able to
Print out a letter.

I hope in the future,
Telephones will be more exciting
And even frightening.

Maybe you'll be able to put your hand through,
And take things from the handset
From the person you are speaking to.

Keith Gray (11)
Grange Primary School

TALKING ANIMALS

I wonder if there are going to be
Talking animals? If they are going
To have little machines put
Into them so they can speak.
But anyway, no one will know unless
They die and come back and
Tell us, but it would be a
Wish come true if they did.

Other animals like rabbits and bears
And dogs etc, etc, they would have
To get special buttons for
Their machines where they can
Tell you what they want and
Where to get it.

Little baby animals would
Not be able to get
Machines put into them because
They would still be fragile
And their bones could break easily.

If there were more animals
That talk, the world would
Be full of animals that
Love to speak and tell you
What they want.

Lesley-Anne Hutchens (10)
Grange Primary School

CLASSROOM 2020

No jotters, a PC instead,
You don't need to draw and paint,
Typing away on computers all day,
Games on it that we can play.

No teacher, just a robot,
It could be old or new,
It will not shout as much,
As many teachers do.

Lots of children in a classroom,
Hardly any now,
We read storybooks,
They will listen to them.

Aisha Ahmed (10)
Grange Primary School

THE STREAM

You are wide in the middle,
Thin at the top,
Sometimes you turn, sometimes you're straight,
The higher we go the faster you get,
The slippery rock and damp moss you make,
The marshy muddy ground you drown,
You've changed the land,
Some is rain, the rest is fresh
In that small clear spring,
but
In a way you're slowly dying.

Alan Manthorpe (10)
Gullane Primary School

UP IN THE HILLS

Up in the hills of Lammermuirs
I see villages so small
They remind me
Of a little toy settlement.

Up in the hills
I see heather so sweet
Like a see on the hills
As colourful as a perfect picture.

Up in the hills
I hear nothing
It is as quiet as a star at night
That shines so bright.

Up in the hills
I hear the laughter of my friends
As I listen to the sounds
In the tranquil Lammermuir hills.

Russell Gardiner (11)
Gullane Primary School

HILLWALKING

Blue skies filled with joy,
Clear water you could drink,
Slippery, wet rocks we climb,
The boiling sun
Sweat running down my cheeks.

Fresh air with fresh water,
Muddy paths, rocky paths,
People shouting with joy,
Bones of poor animals,
Spiky old bushes pricking you.

The stream flows quickly down the hill,
People start to drink out of you,
People throw stones at you,
Big hills, small hills,
People throwing the frisbee with joy.

Lying in the soft heather,
Get back to the minibus eventually,
Now we say goodbye.

Kevin Smith (10)
Gullane Primary School

THE HILLY HEAVENS

Sizzling sun, shining down
on Highland heather,
On top of the hill, feeling
toasted from the torturing sun.
Land so beautiful,
Air so sweet
No noise, just wind,
Day goes on and on,
So fresh the water.

Helping hands,
Helpful in hard parts,
Love the land,
Life so sweet.

Duncan Melville (10)
Gullane Primary School

LONELINESS

He sits there gloomily in his wheelchair,
    Feeling embarrassed as people stare,
He talks about good times long long ago,
    As the effects of disease now painfully show.

His limp hands drop against any effort he makes,
    The hands that used to roam flat landscapes,
His golfing legs are useless now,
    He cannot play even though he knows how.

The worries of death come nearer and press,
    And the bills of the Nursing Home bring more and more stress,
He says 'Now no one does a thing that I say'
    When we are trying our best to get things his way.

He tries his best to make everyone laugh,
    But his jokes don't appeal to other patients or staff,
He tells us stories of times in the past,
    He does not understand that good things don't last.

But still he's my grandpa and love him I will,
    Seeing him suffer cuts my heart like a drill,
I have to accept he won't be the same, never,
    Will he be lonely for ever and ever?

Catherine Holme (10)
Gullane Primary School

THE RIVER

The moving mingling river
Runs merrily through the hills
A rat's tail all cold and wet
Looking out to sea so blue.

The binding burly bird
To us has such a voice
Finely he ducks and dives
In soft warm heather.

The high heathery hills
Covered from head to toe
So beautiful and alive
Looks up to the bright background.

Jenny McPhail (10)
Gullane Primary School

THE MILLENNIUM BOX

I would like to put in my box and bury:
The gold coin I found when I was down in England.
The Cub badge that will remind me of when I was in the Cubs.
The smell of broken up biscuits in a pet shop.
The sound of a bus on the motorway.
The touch of my cousin's gerbil as it runs along my hands.
The smell of spicy crinkle chips.
The feel of a rabbit's smooth fur.
The sizzling sound of smoky sausages
And the grin of giggling girls.

Aaron Paddon (9)
Kinneil Primary School

MY MILLENNIUM WISH

My millennium wish would be that there would be
No more wars all over the world.
Or beggars begging for money.
Not to see bombs dropping anywhere and big clouds of smoke.
Nor poison or pollution spoiling the water and birds covered in oil.
No more sound of guns banging on and on.
Or the saws cutting down trees.
And no more students struggling with fees.
My wish would be to see children
Chatting happily on their way to school.
Tall trees growing everywhere.
I would like to see homeless people being housed.
And landmines being cleared.
This is my wish for the millennium.

Stephen Kernaghan (9)
Kinneil Primary School

MY MILLENNIUM WISH

My wish for the millennium would be that there would be
No more ragged beggars.
No more sounds of warring and no more goose-stepping soldiers.
No more coloured people being called names.
And that plants, birds, animals and people could be cared for.
My wish would be that children everywhere are educated.
Swans could swim safely in ponds.
And I could listen to the stillness of silent guns.

Leanne Acres (9)
Kinneil Primary School

MY MILLENNIUM WISH

My millennium wish would be that there would be no more beggars
pleading for money
And no more landmines being made.
To see old folk able to turn the heating on without worrying about
the cost.
No more sound of bombs blowing up,
Or the smell of forests being burned down,
Or the need for burglar alarms and security lights.
My millennium wish is to hear chubby children chattering.
Strong soldiers safe with bombs being banned forever
And perfect peace all over the world.

Gemma Brand (9)
Kinneil Primary School

MY MILLENNIUM WISH

My millennium wish would be that there would be
No more homeless people.
Nor bombs being dropped.
No more dirty and hungry children
Nor refugees sleeping rough.
No more sounds of bombs being dropped and
No more landmines exploding.
My wish would be to see swans swimming safely in a pond.
Every child in a happy home.
People being able to have confidence in themselves.
Then the world would be a better place.

Ann-Marie McLean (9)
Kinneil Primary School

MY MILLENNIUM WISH

My millennium wish would be that there would be no more
Soldiers shooting with savage stenguns.
Old folk dying of illnesses or diseases.
Beggars begging for money.
Children having to go out to work.
Fish fighting for life,
Or bird's eggs being taken by collectors.
My wish is to see
Soldiers coming home from war and never returning.
Old folk sitting rocking in rocking chairs,
Or beggars being able to buy a house.
Children chomping on candy canes,
And fish swimming happily in the sea.
In the millennium, I hope my wish will come true.

Stewart Murdoch (9)
Kinneil Primary School

THE MILLENNIUM BOX

I would like to put in my box and bury
My raggy old burst ball.
And my newest, noisiest Sega game.
The first picture I drew.
The smell of swimsuits,
And the sound of the roar at Ibrox.
The taste of the cleanest water in the world.

Adam King (9)
Kinneil Primary School

THE AUTUMN LADY

In summer she is frisky,
Alive and full.
But autumn is approaching.
The nights are drawing in,
The great autumn ball is near.
She's preparing her ball gown,
Her leaves turning scarlet, gold and russet.
Splashes of colour on her slender trunk.

Winter is now approaching,
The ball is past.
It's winter.
Her gown has gone,
She can feel the icy breath of death.
But deep, deep down there is still a little life,
Silent till spring.

Alison Shepherd (11)
Prestonfield School

THE SNOW QUEEN

A beautiful sight of shivering white,
As she danced through the night.
Upon her dress, shapes great and small,
All coloured in sparkling white.
A fragment of thin ice.
As the queen, she ruled the skies.
She danced with the morning sun
And disappeared in light,
Leaving a blanket
Where she had lain for the night.

Louise Manson (11)
Prestonfield School

THE HAUNTED HOUSE

The wind whirls round the empty house,
Where everything lies still,
Nothing lives and nothing moves,
In this house on the eerie hill.

Cobwebs hang in each corner,
But no one will clear them away,
Because no one has visited this house,
Since the hauntings of that day.

The day the ghosts appeared,
With a terrible wailing sound,
All the people living there
Disappeared and were never found.

Because, before the house was built,
This hill was the witches' own,
But with the house came people
And the witches were not alone.

As darkness falls on Hallowe'en,
The witches return to this site,
Their meeting ground for many years,
They're haunting again tonight.

Donald Chapman (11)
Prestonfield School

THE WINTER OF MY LIFE

It's freezing outside.
The cold . . .
It numbs my hands and makes it hard to move.
My breath comes in painful, short gasps.
I see my breath turn to frost in front of me.
The wind is so powerful,
I have to stop myself being blown over
by clinging to walls.
I look at my gnarled hands and think,
'When did I turn so old?'
I hear children having fun in the snow.
'I used to have fun in the snow', I thought.
The children played happily,
winter is not a happy time for me.

Tariq Ashkanani (11)
Prestonfield School

WINTER

Winter is a time to sit around the fire,
The poor animals
Hoping their coats keep them warm.
The bleak streets
Look like clouds from the sky.
People's washing
Camouflaged by the snow.
Children throwing snowballs.
The snow is like crystal,
The bitterness and cold.
Birds flock to hotter climates,
Snowmen feel warm,
But Jack Frost will always be about.

Dean Shanks (12)
Prestonfield School

MY WAR

I hear the bombing of houses
Screams of young children,
As I wait cold and silently
In the air raid shelter,
I hear fear

I see rubble of bombed buildings
Some people lying injured,
Some even dead
Families crying over loved ones
And bombs about to explode.
I want to see none of this,
But I see people in misery.

I smell burning and smoke
As though I am on fire
Gas leaking
I smell a war.

I taste smoke
But I taste no food
Rations are low
I can taste the end.
I feel pain
And loneliness
I am feeling more pain than ever before,
But now I feel my death.

Helen Brannigan (11)
Prestonfield School

WINTER

As the snow falls every year
We get frostbite on our ears
People stranded in the snow
As the blizzards blow and blow

Snow and ice lying thick
As trees and cables fall like sticks
People with no light and heat
Ending up with frozen feet

Sledging is such fun for kids
Skating and sliding into skids
Making snowmen as they go
Throwing snowballs to and fro

While all the children scream and run
Not all God's creatures have such fun
The animals and birds, they scrape and flap
And fight each other for every scrap.

Donna Johnston (11)
Prestonfield School

WORRY

Worry is white.
It tastes of salt
and the smell of burnt toast.
It looks like swirls of smoke
and it sounds like people speaking and annoying you.
Worry feels like air going through your hair very fast.

Louise Malcolm (11)
St Mary's RC Primary School, Bonnyrigg

ODE TO A DEAD MOUSE

Blackie Mouse, I loved you,
Your long pink tail,
And short sharp nail,
You were the best,
With your little straw nest.

Blackie Mouse, I loved you,
Your little white teeth,
I would have called you Keith,
Your black fur,
Made me call you Blackie.

Blackie Mouse, I loved you,
With your little pink shoe,
You were always new,
Little tiny bones,
And some constant moods.

Gary Rushforth (10)
St Mary's RC Primary School, Bonnyrigg

IF NIGHT-TIME WAS DAYTIME

If night-time was daytime
I would lie in bed all day
Think about the sunny days
Playing with my friends
Think about the bad days
Listening to the rain
On the windowpane
I wish I could go out to play
But it's not day!

Kayleigh Donnelly (10)
St Mary's RC Primary School, Bonnyrigg

ODE TO A LAZY DOG

Lazy dog I love you
'cause you're my favourite pet
One morning when I got up
you were at the vet

Lazy dog I love you
you're always in my house
You wouldn't dare to scare a cat
but you would just scare a mouse

Lazy dog I love you
'cause you're my favourite pet
Lazy dog I've loved you
from the first day that we met.

Kriss Williamson (10)
St Mary's RC Primary School, Bonnyrigg

ODE TO A LAZY HAMSTER

Lazy hamster I love you,
but do you still love me too.
You are always up at night,
and you give me such a fright.
Lazy hamster I love you.

Lazy hamster I love you,
but do you still love me too.
You're ginger, small and fluffy,
do you know your name is Toffee?
Lazy hamster I love you.

Kirsty Fleming (10)
St Mary's RC Primary School, Bonnyrigg

ODE TO A RABBIT

How I love you rabbit
Your small pink nose, rabbit
Your bobby tail
Your long sharp nail
And your screeching, scratching habit.

How I love you rabbit
Playing games, rabbit
Now you're dead
You have not been fed
Now I miss you rabbit.

Sinead Johnstone (10)
St Mary's RC Primary School, Bonnyrigg

COLD COTTAGE

In a cottage so cold
There lived a woman so old
I wonder how she survives
Bread and butter from the gutter
Toast and jam and maybe ham
A lady from a cold cottage
Throughout all the lands
That's where she stands
In the grass with no gas
Washing and hoovering with no water
A lady from a cold cottage.

Leona Johnstone (7)
St Mary's RC Primary School, Bonnyrigg

THE CREAKY HOUSE

We live in a creaky house.

Every night there is a robber
No there's not! It's the floorboards.

Every night there's a fire
No there's not! It's the water bottle.

Every morning there's a leak
No there's not! It's the bath running.

Every night someone is in the fridge
No there's not! It's dad coming in from the pub.

Every night there is someone on my bed
No there's not! It's the cat.

Every night there is someone snoring
No there's not! It's the dog.

Michael Allan (10)
St Mary's RC Primary School, Bonnyrigg

FEAR

Fear is blue,
it tastes like freezing cold ice
and smells like a winter night.
Fear looks like a horrible nightmare
and sounds like teeth chattering.
Fear is a test that makes you cry.

Stevie Gillies (10)
St Mary's RC Primary School, Bonnyrigg

JULIA

My friend Julia,

has ringlets in her hair, her hair is blonde,
sea blue eyes,
likes eating healthy things like fruit and salad,
likes playing on her bike,
likes playing Red Letter.
Julia is very thin,
likes being kind and helpful.
Julia is always there to talk to when you are upset,
always telling jokes and being funny.

Sarah Mills (10)
St Mary's RC Primary School, Bonnyrigg

COMPUTERS!

Computers, computers they're so hard,
even to make a birthday card.
Click, clack I think I'm going mad,
click, clack, clack on the keypad.
I think it is confusing,
hope you don't bother me 'cause I'm fuming.
I think I'm going insane,
hope no one bothers me again.
Echoes running through my head,
bye-bye, see ya, I'm going to bed.

Nathan Campbell Anderson (10)
St Mary's RC Primary School, Bonnyrigg

HAPPINESS

Happiness is purple

It tastes of strawberries, sugar and cream
and smells like a red rose.

Happiness looks like a warm, sandy beach
it feels warm and cosy.

Happiness is a paddling pool in summer,
that makes you laugh.

Lauren Fenty (10)
St Mary's RC Primary School, Bonnyrigg

HAPPINESS

Happiness is a light blue.
It tastes like sugar
and smells like perfume.
Happiness looks like children playing
and sounds like people laughing.
Happiness feels like a sunny day.

Rachel Murphy (10)
St Mary's RC Primary School, Bonnyrigg

MOTHER

You're Miss Montgomery to many
You're known as Annie to some
But to me you will
Always be my wonderful, lovely
    Old Mum.

Lauren Montgomery (10)
St Mary's RC Primary School, Bonnyrigg

IF NIGHT WAS ONLY DAY

If night was only day I could read
or play
Or watch TV and play with toys
and chatter with the boys
If night was only day
I would go out and play
Play hide and seek and go to school
see my friends at the pool.

Laura Cryans (10)
St Mary's RC Primary School, Bonnyrigg

MY MUM

My mum always shouts
'Did you check your hamster Lesley-anne?'
And I say 'Yes Mum, I did check my hamster today.'

My mum is very, very, very kind
and very understanding.
She's the best mum in the whole world.

Lesley-Anne Haughton (10)
St Matthew's Primary School, Rosewell

HATE

Hate is black
It tastes like cold porridge
It smells like smoke
It looks like bark
It sounds like the wind
It feels like night

Steven Juner (11)
St Matthew's Primary School, Rosewell

I AM...

I am a pair of fast feet.
I am a pair of juggling hands
I am a pair of looking eyes
I am a pair of listening ears.

I am a jolly joker
I am an animal lover
I am an exquisite eater
I am a frenzied footballer

I am a tennis terror
I am a sporty swimmer
I am a curious cub
I am a Yomega yo-yoer.

That's me!

Paolo Tamburrini (8)
St Peter's RC Primary School, Edinburgh

I AM...

I am a pair of laughing, brown eyes,
I am a pair of cracking teeth,
I am a pair of chatting lips,
I am a pair of listening ears.

I am a pair of dancing feet,
I am a pair of jumping legs
I am a pair of football boots,
I am a Karate kicker.

That's me!

Chris Motion (9)
St Peter's RC Primary School, Edinburgh

I AM...

I am a pair of listening ears
I am a pair of hazel eyes,
I am a pair of fast feet,
I am a pair of sparkling teeth.

I am a rapid reader,
I am a sporty swimmer
I am a poetry pencil writer,
I am an arty, crafty person.

I am an animal lover,
I am a jolly joker,
I am a willing worker,
I am a pair of Tracker trainers.

I am a jazzy dancer.

That's me!

Daniela Chianta (8)
St Peter's RC Primary School, Edinburgh

I AM...

I am a pair of bright blue eyes
I am a pair of fast feet
I am a brave, booming boy
I am a pair of gripping hands

I am a dazzling drummer
I am a cuddly dog lover
I am a buzzing bee
I am a frenzied footballer

That's me!

Shaun Nicol (8)
St Peter's RC Primary School, Edinburgh

I AM . . .

I am a pair of dark brown eyes,
I am a pair of chatting lips,
I am a pair of fast feet,
I am a mouth of laughing teeth.

I am a dog lover,
I am an arty girl,
I am a sporty swimmer,
I am a pair of dancing feet.

I am a pair of fiddly fingers,
I am a pair of looking eyes,
I am a little monster,
I am a sporty girl.

That's me!

Kimberley Harris (8)
St Peter's RC Primary School, Edinburgh

I AM . . .

I am a pair of hazel eyes,
I am a pair of jumping feet,
I am a head of fuzzy, wuzzy hair,
I am a pair of floppy hands.

I am a jolly joker,
I am a pair of fast feet,
I am a pair of funny ears,
I am a pair of blinking eyes.

I am a pair of sporty knees.

That's me!

Danielle Randall (8)
St Peter's RC Primary School, Edinburgh

I AM . . .

I am a pair of chewing teeth
I am a pair of looking eyes
I am a pair of running feet
I am a pair of clapping hands

I am a shy snail
I am a sporty swimmer
I am a buzzing bee
I am a recipe reader

I am a dizzy dancer
I am a sweet, sweet eater
I am a problem, poem writer
I am a famous footballer

That's me!

Sarah Pickering (9)
St Peter's RC Primary School, Edinburgh

I AM . . .

I am a pair of fiddly hands
I am a high, high climber
I am a cracking joker
I am a jolly jumper

I am a dazzling drawer
I am a pair of fast feet
I am a pair of clean teeth
I am a bouncy basketball player

That's me!

Dean Lynch (8)
St Peter's RC Primary School, Edinburgh

I AM . . .

I am a glittering goalkeeper
I am a pair of blue eyes
I am a pair of catching hands
I am a pair of non-stop feet

I am a long sleeper
I am a Man U maniac
I am a frenzied footballer
I am a compact computer

I am a chasing cheetah
I am a laughing lion
I am a bouncing basketball player
I am a drumming drummer

That's me!

Jamie Vernon (8)
St Peter's RC Primary School, Edinburgh

I AM . . .

I am a pair of fast feet
I am a pair of clean teeth
I am a pair of blue eyes
I am a head of blonde hair

I am an animal lover
I am a cracking drawer
I am a jolly joker
I am a high climber

That's me!

Emma Finnie (9)
St Peter's RC Primary School, Edinburgh

I AM...

I am a pair of fiddly fingers
I am a pair of funny feet
I am a mouth of sweet teeth
I am a pair of sore knees

I am a sporty footballer
I am an arty boy
I am a big, bold writer
I am a little monster

That's me!

Michael MacKay (9)
St Peter's RC Primary School, Edinburgh

I AM...

I am a pair of green eyes
I am a head of brown hair
I am a pair of humming feet
I am a pair of tasty teeth

I am a dizzy dancer
I am a gleaming, glossy person
I am a smarty, arty, kind of person
I am a very funny bunny

That's me!

Jasmine Cochrane (9)
St Peter's RC Primary School, Edinburgh

I AM...

I am a pair of dark brown eyes
I am a pair of excellent ears
I am a pair of tasty teeth
I am a pair of horror hands

I am a dazzling dancer
I am a glorious gymnast
I am a terrific tennis player
I am an ace actor

I am a super-duper singer

That's me!

Claire Hennigan (8)
St Peter's RC Primary School, Edinburgh

I AM...

I am a pair of bright blue eyes
I am a pair of buzzy feet
I am a pair of catching hands
I am a pair of big toes

I am a dog lover
I am a football lover
I am a munching mouth
I am a sporting boy

That's me!

Nathan Hill (9)
St Peter's RC Primary School, Edinburgh

I AM...

I am a pair of tasty teeth
I am a pair of flopping feet
I am a pair of blue eyes
I am a pair of listening ears

I am a brown haired girl
I am a buzzing bee
I am a jazzy dancer
And I am a sleepy snoozer

That's me!

Amy Dolan (8)
St Peter's RC Primary School, Edinburgh

I AM...

I am a pair of blue eyes
I am a pair of football feet
I am a buzzing bee
I am a pair of jumping feet

I am a pair of running feet
I am a super swimmer
I am a pair of walking feet
I am a pair of hopping feet

That's me!

Graham Cairns (8)
St Peter's RC Primary School, Edinburgh

WHAT IS THE SUN?

The Sun is a giant blow fish
swimming to the clouds.
It is an orange beach ball
thrown to outer space.

The Sun is a hot sunflower
blown off its roots.
It is a dandelion
gliding through space.

The Sun is a yellow ball
drawn in the sky.
It is a red ball
flying in the sky.

David McBride (8)
St Peter's RC Primary School, Edinburgh

I AM . . .

I am a pair of brown eyes
I am a pair of floppy hands
I am a pair of fast feet
I am a jolly joker

I am a wazzy, dazzy, football player
I am a karate cracker
I am a pair of jumping feet
I am a baseball wizard

That's me!

Matthew Bell (8)
St Peter's RC Primary School, Edinburgh

WHAT IS THE SUN?

The sun is an orange bauble
blown out the window.
It is a bouncing ball
flying in outer space.

Arianna Moran (9)
St Peter's RC Primary School, Edinburgh

WHAT IS THE SUN?

The sun is a giant sunflower
lighting up the land.
It is a big, juicy orange
splitting into many pieces.

Benjamin Brogan (8)
St Peter's RC Primary School, Edinburgh

WHAT IS THE SUN?

The sun is a yellow umbrella
twisting through the air.
It is a golden pendulum ball,
swinging to and fro.

Joshua Barnes (9)
St Peter's RC Primary School, Edinburgh

WHAT IS THE SUN?

The sun is a light bulb
glowing in the sky.
It is a beach ball
kicked into the sky.

The sun is a balloon
floating through the air.
It is a golden pancake
flicked into outer space.

The sun is a blow fish
that glows throughout the world.
It is a red bauble
lighting up the sky.

Patrick Buglass (9)
St Peter's RC Primary School, Edinburgh

THE SUN

The sun is a yellow beach ball
kicked high in the sky.
It is an unknown planet
drifting in outer space.

The sun is a golden marshmallow
flipped in the air.
It is an orange star
stuck there so high.

Liam Rafferty (8)
St Peter's RC Primary School, Edinburgh

WHAT IS THE SUN?

The sun is a yellow beach ball,
kicked up into space.
It is a light bulb
shining on my face.

Joshua Robinson (8)
St Peter's RC Primary School, Edinburgh

WHAT IS THE SUN?

The sun is a big beach ball
going around the world.
It is a giant gobstopper
rolling through the sky.

Rachael Quinn
St Peter's RC Primary School, Edinburgh

WHAT IS THE SUN?

The sun is a light bulb
glowing up in the sky.
It is a golden sphere
lighting up the sky.

Peter Daly (8)
St Peter's RC Primary School, Edinburgh

WHAT IS THE SUN?

The sun is a golden light bulb
lighting up the sky.
It is a swinging sphere
rocking side to side.

The sun is a hot sunflower
shining above the clouds.
It is a yellow bouncy ball
spinning round and round.

The sun is a red gobstopper
gleaming through the sky.
It is a flying saucer
staying as still as it can.

The sun is a coloured bubble
far up in the sky.
It is a golden pancake
tossed above the hills.

Catherine Oliver (8)
St Peter's RC Primary School, Edinburgh

WHAT IS THE SUN?

The sun is an orange football
kicked into outer space.
It is a giant basketball
bouncing off the clouds.

Michael Kelly (9)
St Peter's RC Primary School, Edinburgh

WHAT IS THE SUN?

The sun is a beautiful sunflower
lighting up the earth.
It is a giant orange
bobbing in the air.

The sun is a yellow wheel
whirling through the sky.
It is a golden ball of wool
spinning round and round.

The sun is a splendid sparkler
spitting out its rays.
It is an unknown planet
floating in outer space.

Riccardo Alonzi (8)
St Peter's RC Primary School, Edinburgh

WHAT IS THE SUN?

The sun is a glowing ball
bouncing through the sky.
It is an orange lolly
peeking through the clouds.

The sun is a yellow light bulb
dazzling over there.
It is a red goldfish
sparkling everywhere.

Thomas Ball (8)
St Peter's RC Primary School, Edinburgh

WHAT IS THE SUN?

The sun is a yellow beach ball
bounced into the sky.
It is a golden circle
coloured by a magic pen.

The sun is a yellow pizza
spun into heaven high.
It is an orange, orange,
thrown into the blue.

The sun is a burning ball
whooshed into the clouds.
It is a red gobstopper
spat out through the world.

Sophie Walker (9)
St Peter's RC Primary School, Edinburgh

WHAT AM I?

I fly through the sky like a bird,
I save people's lives like a ranger,
I dive under water like a diver,
I have a fin like a shark,
What am I?
A dolphin.

I come in every colour and size,
I slither through the grass,
I have fangs the size of a nail.
I can kill in any way.
What am I?
A snake.

Luke Guiot (8)
St Peter's RC Primary School, Edinburgh

WHAT IS THE SUN?

The sun is a light bulb
lighting up the world.
It is a robin's breast
gleaming in the sky.

The sun is a leopard's golden fur
dazzling the ground below.
It is a sandy beach
covering the sky above.

The sun is a star
shining through the mist.
It is a firework
bursting across the sky.

The sun is a ball of fire
everlasting all day long.
It is a colourful butterfly
spreading out its wings.

Matthew Benson (9)
St Peter's RC Primary School, Edinburgh

WHAT IS THE SUN?

The sun is a golden dandelion
dancing through the sky.
It is a bright flower
spreading its petals high.

The sun is a yellow firework
shooting into space.
It is an orange beach ball
a bright, smiling face.

Polly Reaves (8)
St Peter's RC Primary School, Edinburgh

WHAT IS THE SUN?

The sun is a glittering sunflower
swaying in the sky.
It is an orange gobstopper,
floating very high.

The sun is a yellow beach ball,
which someone threw away.
It is a giant apple,
shining throughout the day.

The sun is a dazzling light bulb,
lighting up the sky.
It is a golden penny,
stuck way up high.

Alison McNaughton (8)
St Peter's RC Primary School, Edinburgh

WHAT IS THE SUN?

The sun is a bright dandelion,
brightening up the garden.
It is a golden sunflower
smiling to the people.

The sun is an orange gobstopper
kicked up in the sky.
It is a golden pancake
floating through the air.

James Murphy (9)
St Peter's RC Primary School, Edinburgh

WHAT IS THE SUN?

The sun is a glittering ball,
sparkling through the sky.
It is an orange globe
hanging through the air.

The sun is a yellow diamond
dazzling in the sky.
It is a glowing bauble
swinging to and fro.

The sun is a juicy orange
squashed between the clouds.
It is a yellow tennis ball
smashed across the land.

Brendan Friel (8)
St Peter's RC Primary School, Edinburgh

WHAT IS THE SUN?

The sun is a gleaming dial
working across the sky.
It is a golden daisy
opening after the night.

The sun is a shining king
gleaming down on earth.
It is a giant pancake
glowing in outer space.

The sun is a scrumptious sweet
making the clouds hungry.
It is a yellow goldfish
swimming in the air.

Stephen Jarvie (8)
St Peter's RC Primary School, Edinburgh